PENGUIN BOOKS

CUBA

Alan Twigg is now writing *Belize: A Concise History for Travelers*. His previous six books include *Vancouver & Its Writers, Strong Voices: Conversations with Fifty Canadian Authors* and *Vander Zalm: From Immigrant to Premier*. He lives in Vancouver.

CUBA

A Concise History for Travelers

Alan Twigg

Penguin Books

PENGUIN BOOKS

Published by the Penguin Group

Penguin Books Canada Ltd, 10 Alcorn Avenue, Toronto, Ontario, Canada M4V
    3B2

Penguin Books Ltd, 80 Strand, London WC2R 0RL, England

Penguin Putnam Inc., 375 Hudson Street, New York, New York 10014, U.S.A.

Penguin Books Australia Ltd, 250 Camberwell Road, Camberwell, Victoria 3124,
    Australia

Penguin Books (NZ) Ltd, cnr Rosedale and Airborne Roads, Albany, Auckland
    1310, New Zealand

Penguin Books Ltd, Registered Offices: Harmondsworth, Middlesex, England

First published by Bluefield Books, 2000
Published in Penguin Books, 2002

10 9 8 7 6 5 4 3 2 1

Most interior photos of Cuba by Alan Twigg. Photos of exhibits in museums were
taken with permission and/or payment, 1998–2000.

Manufactured in Canada.

NATIONAL LIBRARY OF CANADA CATALOGUING IN PUBLICATION DATA

Twigg, Alan, 1952–
   Cuba : a concise history for travelers

ISBN 0-14-301235-5

1. Cuba—History. I. Title.

F1776.T84   2002   972.91   C2001-902681-1

Visit Penguin Canada's website at **www.penguin.ca**

CONTENTS

CUBA

1 | A SPANISH COLONY

Cuba has been a four-letter word for too long.

—CUBAN PLAYWRIGHT DOLORES PRIDA

Kept in Baracoa, this carbon-dated cross, reputedly brought by Columbus, is said to be the oldest European relic in the Americas

CRISTOFORO COLOMBO OF GENOA sailed westward from the Spanish port of Palos on August 3, 1492, looking for the continent of Asia. After stopping at the Canary Islands, he navigated three ships across the Atlantic and quelled a mutiny attempt on the *Santa María* on October 10, promising his crew they could sail back to Spain if land was not sighted in three more days.

"A little branch full of dog roses" floated by. Two nights later, near daybreak, one of his lookouts on the *Pinta,* Rodrigo Berguemo of Triana, saw the silhouette of an island in the moonlight. Columbus named it San Salvador (now Watling Island in the Bahamas). The natives were friendly but Columbus didn't tarry. "I did not wish to stop, in order to discover and search many islands to find gold."

More than five centuries later, a remarkable story of cruelty and endurance may be told.

CUBA'S FIRST TOURIST

Columbus first saw Cuba, the largest island in the Caribbean, on October 27, 1492. He proclaimed it "the loveliest land that human

eyes have beheld, a land to be desired, and once seen, never to be left, with palm leaves so big they can roof a house and always the same deafening symphony from the songs of birds."

Columbus is presumed to have first touched land near Gibara, on the northeast coast, then stayed a week near the eastern end of Cuba, at the present site of Baracoa, beginning on November 27, with two of his three

Columbus in Baracoa

ships. (The captain of the *Pinta*, in an act of "treachery," had sailed off from the main party on November 20, and he reunited with Columbus on January 6, off Hispaniola.)

Hoping that he had reached the Chinese continent, Columbus was delighted to learn about an inland city, Cubanacan, where he thought the Great Khan might reside. He believed he had found a route to the Indies and therefore referred to the local people as Indians.

"They are the best people in the world, without knowledge of what is evil; nor do they murder or steal. All the people show the most singular loving behaviour and are gentle and always laughing. Ten Christians could put 10,000 of them to flight, so cowardly and timid are they."

Columbus's journal also recorded encounters with "men who had only one eye, and others who had a snout of a dog and who fed on human flesh." These were likely the Caribes, much feared by the more peaceful Taino.

Columbus would claim he'd been only a few days' journey from the River Ganges and that he had discovered King Solomon's mines. For the rest of his days he would insist he had reached the East Indies and he regretted he was never able to convert the Chinese emperor to Christianity.

To claim the New World for Spain and Christ, Columbus erected crosses throughout his journey. One of these, the "Cross of Parra," was found 19 years later, near Baracoa, by the island's original Spanish settlers. Since 1959, the regime of Fidel Castro has been loath to publicize a symbol of Catholic/imperialist oppression, and the cross has been inauspiciously housed in a dilapidated church in Baracoa, with minimal security and without signage.

Skeptics say the cross can't be real, but some scientists say otherwise. At the request of Baracoa historian Dr. Alejandro

Hartmann Matos, the cross was examined by Belgian wood specialist Dr. Roger Dechamps. In 1988 he determined the cross was made of uvilla wood, one of 150 tree varieties in the area. It's been called the Cross of Parra because Columbus reputedly placed it near a parra tree. A sample was carbon-14-dated at the Catholic Universidad de Lobaina La Nueva in Brussels in 1988, and test results, published in European scientific and popular journals, support the claim that the Cross of Parra is the oldest European relic in all of the Americas.

Prior to Columbus's arrival, the earliest known inhabitants were Ciboneys (or Siboneys) who arrived in Cuba around 1000 B.C. A contingent of Ciboneys, sometimes referred to as Guanahuatabeys, lived in the western edge of the island. As well, the Mayarí first settled in present-day Oriente province between the ninth and eleventh centuries. The first sub-Taino Indians began to migrate from present-day Haiti in the ninth century and easily displaced or subjugated the Ciboneys and Mayarí. More Taino ("good men"), fleeing the fierce Caribes (cannibals) of Haiti, migrated to Cuba in the mid-fifteenth century.

The Taino, originally from the Orinoco basin in Venezuela, were skilled weavers, potters and boat-builders. "They willingly traded everything they had," Columbus reported. "They seemed to be short of everything." If the hosts of Columbus felt the Spanish were lacking anything, it has not been recorded.

These Indians were "well-built with fine bodies and handsome faces neither black nor white." Columbus decided to take some of them to Spain "so that they can learn to speak. They should be good servants and very intelligent, for I have observed that they soon repeat anything that is said to them."

Intent on finding gold, Columbus reached another promising island, *La Isla Española,* later known as Hispaniola, now Haiti and the Dominican Republic. There his largest ship, the *Santa María*, was wrecked on Christmas morning on a reef and abandoned. Returning to Spain with several scantily clad slaves, a dozen parrots, exotic fruits, tobacco, syphilis and very little gold, Columbus was nonetheless received as a hero.

Coincidental with Columbus's first voyage, Spain was eager for colonial expansion. In 1492, after 700 years of religious conflict, Spain had captured the last Muslim fortress in Iberia, Granada, and finally ended Moorish occupation. The explorations of Christopher Columbus, although delusionary, literally gave the Spanish a new horizon for trade and exploitation. The Portuguese, who were superior navigators, already controlled trade on the West African coast; the Turks were blocking access to the Orient via the Mediterranean; the "new world" to the west would be available for plundering on a first-come, first-served basis. Columbus avidly advertised. "A thousand tongues would not suffice to describe the things of novelty and beauty I saw," he reported.

Queen Isabella and King Ferdinand hastened to establish sovereignty over the Bahamas, Cuba and Hispaniola. In response, Pope Alexander VI issued a papal bull in May of 1493 granting control of all territories found west of the Cape Verde Islands to Spain. Portugal would receive control of any new lands found to the east. The pope's arbitrary dividing line drawn through the Atlantic Ocean, from the North Pole to the South Pole, was moved slightly westward by the Treaty of Tordesillas. This change would give control of South America's largest country, Brazil, to the Portuguese, who first reached Brazil on April 22, 1500.

In return for territorial rights, Spain and Portugal were expected to convert the native inhabitants to Christianity. The Taino, Columbus claimed, could "easily be made Christians."

Europeans flocked to see Columbus's parade of captives who "appeared to have no religion."

One of the Taino kept by the Spanish court reportedly died of sadness after two years in captivity.

Within 100 years of making contact with Columbus, the indigenous people of Cuba, as a race, would be virtually eliminated. This genocide was only partially caused by the spread of new diseases. Columbus, the first *conquistador,* brought with him religious intolerance born of Christian fanaticism. The fall of Constantinople in 1453 and the start of the Spanish Inquisition in 1480 had already made life increasingly dangerous for all heretics and infidels; in 1484 Pope Innocent VIII had issued his bull against witchcraft. In the same year as Columbus's historic first voyage, all Jews had been expelled from Spain. Racial bigotry would give rise to unprecedented cruelty and mass murder.

In 1493, on his second of four voyages, Columbus brought Spanish settlers on 17 ships from Cadiz, introducing sugarcane to Hispaniola. He made all his men take an oath that Cuba was not an island and that they were within reach of China. During this second trip to Cuba, Columbus organized military campaigns against the indigenous population, forced the Taino to pay tributes and transported hundreds of natives to Spain for sale as slaves, but never found the fortune in gold that he craved. His final two expeditions to the coasts of Venezuela and Central America (1498) and the West Indies (1502) were equally disappointing for him. Columbus died in Spain in 1506, at age 55, discredited and disheartened.

The following year a German cartographer published a map that identified the new western lands as "America." This appellation honoured a scholarly Italian, Amerigo Vespucci, who had sailed to the Caribbean as a privileged passenger. Amerigo Vespucci's reports had circulated in Europe prior to the publication of Columbus's journals. "I have found, in these southern lands, a continent," Vespucci wrote. "One can, with good reason, name it the New World."

BARBARISM AND PROGRESS

By 1503 it became necessary for a "board of trade" in Seville, called *Casa de Contración,* to control trade with the Spanish Indies.

In 1508 Sebastian de Ocampo circumnavigated Cuba, proving it was an island, and returned to Spain with rumours of gold.

In 1509 King Ferdinand appointed Columbus's son, Diego, as governor of the Indies.

In 1511 Diego Velázquez was sent from Hispaniola to conquer and explore Cuba. His four ships brought 300 settlers, including Diego Columbus's beautiful wife, Maria de Toledo, who was a grandniece of the Spanish king, as well as an ambitious secretary to the governor, Hernán Cortéz.

A Velázquez Museum in Santiago recreates his home

Arriving at the eastern end of Cuba in October, Velázquez founded the first Spanish town of Baracoa, the oldest colonial settlement in the Americas after Santo Domingo. Here the first European-style marriage ceremony in the Americas was consecrated between Velázquez and Juana de Cuellar, the daughter of a Santo Domingo administrator from Hispaniola, in 1512. She died one week later.

In Baracoa, Velázquez encountered fierce opposition from the Taino, led by a chieftain named Hatuey. Having fled from the Spaniards in Hispaniola, Hatuey had come to Cuba to forewarn the Taino of Spanish cruelty. As such, Hatuey is honoured as Cuba's first "internationalist," forerunner of the Argentinean Che Guevara, and the first of Cuba's many martyrs for freedom.

Research in the 1980s by Dr. Hortencia Pichardo in the Seville archives has proved that Hatuey was not killed in Baracoa, as was commonly believed. Archaeologists and historians concluded Hatuey must have fled west by canoe, intending to alert and possibly mobilize the large Taino settlement near Bayamo. He was captured near Bayamo, at Yara.

As recorded by Bartolomé de las Casas, Hatuey was offered baptism prior to his execution, whereupon Hatuey asked if there would be any Spaniards in heaven. When Hatuey heard the answer from the Spanish friar, Father Juan de Tesin, Hatuey asked not to be baptized. He said if there were Christians in heaven, he preferred to go to hell.

Hatuey was burned at the stake on February 2, 1512. The name Hatuey has been immortalized by a popular brand of beer in Cuba; an American brand of Hatuey beer is also brewed by the Indian Head Brewery in Baltimore, Maryland, backed by the Bacardi empire and primarily sold to anti-Castro Cubans living in Florida.

On December 12, 1512, King Ferdinand thanked Diego Velázquez for conquering Cuba and also for his "humane treatment of the natives." Having eliminated Hatuey, Velázquez and his men established six more outposts of empire at—in order—Bayamo, Trinidad, Sancti Spiritus, Havana, Puerto Principe (modern-day Camaguey) and Santiago de Cuba. But they encountered resistance.

After Hatuey was killed, Guama, the local Taino chieftain in Baracoa, became Cuba's first indigenous resistance leader. Guama held the Spanish under siege in their forts at Baracoa and Puerto Principe. He then took refuge in the same mountains in eastern Cuba from which José Martí and Fidel Castro would organize their revolutionary forces centuries later.

In 1513 Nuñez de Balboa reached the Pacific Ocean overland via Panama. Francisco Pizarro, a peasant-born member of Balboa's trek to the Pacific, would viciously conquer the Incas with only a handful of men and be named governor and captain-general of Peru, in 1528.

Cuba's first great martyr, Hatuey, is honoured with a beer brand

In 1519, at the age of 34, Hernán Cortéz, the first mayor of Santiago de Cuba, sailed from Cuba to conquer Mexico. Well-educated and charming, he became the first of many Spaniards to use Cuba as a base for ruthless plundering expeditions. Cortéz was named governor and captain-general of New Spain in 1522.

Velázquez, as the first governor of Cuba, had granted Spanish settlers the right to force Cuba's indigenous people to work for them. In theory the Taino were supplying their labour in return for Christian teachings; in practice they were worked to death. Many natives chose suicide.

A priest who accompanied Velázquez wrote, "the Devill put himselfe into the Spaniards, to put them all to the edge of the sword in my presence, without any cause whatsoever, more than three thousand soules, which were set before us, men, women and children. I saw there so great cruelties, that never any man living either have or shall see the like."

The most important witness to the devastating cruelty of the Spanish was the "Apostle of the Indies," Fray Bartolomé de las Casas (1474–1566), the first priest to be consecrated in the Spanish West Indies. Born in Seville, he was the son of one of Columbus's navigators on the first voyage to the Americas.

Fray Bartolomé was initially a landowner with slaves. Outraged by the sufferings of the Indians, he returned to Spain and pleaded for mercy from King Ferdinand. "The Indians receive worse treatment than the manure dropped on the plazas," he wrote. Named "Protector General to the Indians," he initially urged for the importation of black slaves and Moors to relieve the plight of the Indians. He would live to deeply regret it.

De las Casas documented the butchery of the Spanish in his book *History of the Indies*. "No tongue is capable of describing to the life all the horrid villainies perpetrated by these bloody-minded men," he wrote. According to de las Casas, the Spanish "thought nothing of knifing Indians by tens and twenties and of cutting slices off them to test the sharpness of their blades." He describes how some Spanish on an expedition, having been fed by the Indians, "slashed, disembowelled and slaughtered the Indians until the blood ran like a river."

Indians were used as food for dogs. For sport and mockery, the Spanish hacked off the hands and feet of Indians before feeding them to their bloodhounds. "It was a fairly common sight to see armies accompanied by processions of slaves chained together to furnish food for the dogs. The more humane of the captains killed them first, but others turned the hungry dogs loose upon the terrified living naked victims."

The people de las Casas tried to protect were "whipped, tortured, castrated, murdered, the women raped, the villages burned, the children left to starve." Forced labour conditions in the mines were lethal.

"The husbands and wives were together only once every eight or ten months and when they met they were so exhausted and depressed on both sides they ceased to procreate. As for the newly born, they died early because their mothers, overworked and famished, had no milk to nurse them, and for this reason, while I was in Cuba, 7,000 children died in three months. Some mothers even drowned their babies in desperation.

"In this way, husbands died in the mines, wives died at work, and children died from lack of milk and in a short time this land which was so great, so powerful and fertile was depopulated. My eyes have seen these acts so foreign to human nature, and now I tremble as I write."

Runaway slaves were tracked by hunting dogs. If recaptured by *ranchadores,* they had an ear cut off. If Spanish soldiers didn't kill the Indians, European diseases did. Their only revenge, in retrospect, was the widespread introduction of tobacco. The Taino smoked the dried leaves of the *cohiba* plant mainly for ceremonial and medicinal purposes. Alarmed by the sudden popularity of tobacco in Europe, the pope tried unsuccessfully to ban smoking in the 1500s.

As the supply of indigenous slaves dwindled, Velázquez imported the first black slaves. Conditions in the Spanish towns and mines gave rise to Cuba's first recorded black slave revolt at Jobabo mines in 1532, the same year the Spanish finally tracked down the whereabouts of Guama and discovered he was already dead. Rebel slaves were decapitated and their heads were displayed as warnings to others.

In 1532 there were still only approximately 500 African slaves in Cuba. In 1538 some black slaves destroyed parts of Havana during an attack by French pirates. Slaves were easily caught and punished; buccaneers less so.

As early as 1523 French pirates had seized some of Cortéz's cargo. In 1555 French pirates and disgruntled slaves under Jacques de Sores captured Havana in less than an hour and demanded ransom. When the Spaniards didn't comply, some were executed.

But the scourge of the Caribbean were the English. Along with France and Holland, England resented the papal edict that had granted the New World to their seafaring rivals, Spain and Portugal. To get their "share" of booty, the English had few qualms about attacking Spanish treasure ships as they departed for Europe. Sponsored by Elizabeth I, in 1580 Francis Drake returned to England in the *Golden Hind,* laden with 26 tons of silver. He received a knighthood.

This ceiba tree in Plaza de Armas marks the founding of Havana in 1519

To combat the menace of pirates like Drake, Christopher Newport, Edward Teach (a.k.a. "Blackbeard"), John Hawkins, Peg-Leg LeClerc, Jean Florin, Gilberto Giró, Chevalier de Gramont and Bartholomew Portugués, the Spanish built fortresses, such as Havana's Castillo de la Real Fuerza.

As the residence for Spanish governors from 1553 to 1762, Castilla de la Real Fuerza was home to Doña Inés de

Bobadilla, Cuba's first female governor. In 1539 she replaced her husband, Hernando de Soto, who had left for Florida to look for the Fountain of Youth. For four years she longed for her husband's return, often gazing out to sea. Her vigil ended with the news that de Soto had been buried on the banks of the Mississippi River. In commemoration of the vigil of Doña Inés de Bobadilla, atop the remains of the castle is a weathervane, *La Giraldilla,* designed in the seventeenth century by Jerónimo Martínez Pinzón and said to symbolize the spirit of Havana. The original *La Giraldilla* is on display at the Havana Museum. It, in turn, was modelled on *La Giralda* at the entrance to Seville harbour.

By mid-century there were only 700 Europeans on the island, and the Spanish had relegated their seven towns in Cuba to serve as supply posts for their more lucrative expeditions in Mexico, Peru and Bolivia. In a period of only 50 years the *conquistadores* completed the "pacification" of Central and South America with the noteworthy exceptions of Brazil and the Argentinian *pampas.*

The Spanish colonial cities that arose in quick succession to compete with Havana and Santiago de Cuba were Mexico City (1521), Quito (1534), Lima (1535), Buenos Aires (1536), Asunción (1537), Sucre (1538), Bogotá (1541), Santiago (1542), Potosi (1545) and La Paz (1548).

Santiago de Cuba in the east of Cuba was named the capital in 1515, but Havana's harbour made it the main transportation depot for riches. Originally named *San Cristobal de Habana,* Havana was at first a modest settlement, established by Panfilo de Narvaez on the south coast of Cuba and reputedly named for a local Indian "princess." The village moved three times until the settlers arrived at Havana Bay in 1519.

Temporarily eclipsed by Portobello in Panama and Veracruz in Mexico, Havana didn't become the capital of Cuba until 1607.

By this time Havana was home to half of the island's 20,000 European inhabitants.

The port established Latin America's first shipyard. The remote and less protected eastern residents of Cuba were resentful of Havana's closer relations to Spain, giving rise to seeds of rebellion throughout Cuba's history.

Although the heart of commerce was Havana, a city officially decreed by the Spanish crown as "the key to the New World" in 1624, the heart of Cuban culture was ethnically diverse Santiago de Cuba, in closer proximity to Hispaniola, homeland of Hatuey. As the island's only official "Hero City," Santiago de Cuba first prospered due to a copper mine that was opened at Cobre, 12 miles to the northwest, in 1530. This mine supplied the ore for Havana's artillery works, the largest munitions base in the New World.

The first European mine in the Western Hemisphere, El Cobre's open-pit mine remains operational near the cathedral. The labour for the Cobre mine was provided by some of the 750,000 slaves imported to Cuba between 1526 and 1867, mainly from the present-day countries of Senegal, Gambia, Guinea, Nigeria and the Congo. (*Monumento al Cimarrón,* a remarkable modernist sculpture by Alberto Lescay, was erected above the mine in 1997 to commemorate runaway slaves and the slaves who had worked and died below. Seed money for the project was provided by a Senegalese employee of UNESCO in Paris, Doudou Dienne, who came to Cuba to make peace with his ancestral past. Both Dienne and Lescay consulted with the local santería *babalawo,* Juan Gonzalez Perez.)

Slave owners bred their slaves like cattle. The average slave labour life span in Cuba during the sixteenth century was seven years, but these slaves nonetheless managed to transfer some of their religious traditions from Africa to their descendants. *Palo Monte,* for instance, is a "black magic" religion in Cuba that emanates from the Congo River region; devotees of the *Abakuá* religion practice all-male rituals that can be traced to parts of Nigeria and Cameroon.

Although marriage was not allowed, tribesmen from West Africa such as the Yoruba, Fulani and Hausa were often kept together rather than divided, giving rise to the santería faith among poor Afro-Cubans. In the twentieth century, santería has served as the most potent alternative system of beliefs to communism and Catholicism.

In the faith of santería, believers use human interpreters called *santeros* to conduct rites of divination, sacrifice, exorcism and initiation. As personifications of the divine and righteous force called *ashe,* oracles called *orishas* are worshipped to please the all-powerful god *Oludamare.* A male medium called a *babalawo* can conduct the most complex ritual, called *ifa,* in which shell patterns are consulted to reveal one of 256 possible combinations. Keeping the immortal *orishas* happy is the basic practice of the faith. When the *babalawos* began to switch their allegiance to Fidel Castro's rebel movement in 1958, the dictator Batista, who had consulted *santeros* for much of his life—he'd grown up poor in eastern Cuba—took it as a sign that he had lost the confidence of the people.

THE VIRGIN OF COPPER

The relocation and subjugation of black slaves and the growth of santería gave rise to Cuba's most sacred image, the *Virgen del Cobre.*

The legend goes that in 1606 two young Indians and a young slave named Juan Moreno found the statue of a *mestizo*

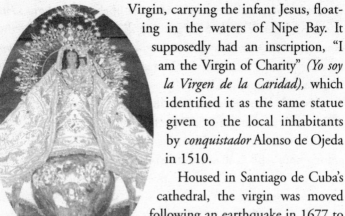

The Virgin of Copper

Virgin, carrying the infant Jesus, float-ing in the waters of Nipe Bay. It supposedly had an inscription, "I am the Virgin of Charity" *(Yo soy la Virgen de la Caridad),* which identified it as the same statue given to the local inhabitants by *conquistador* Alonso de Ojeda in 1510.

Housed in Santiago de Cuba's cathedral, the virgin was moved following an earthquake in 1677 to a sanctuary near the copper mine. There the slaves began to worship the virgin as a spiritual patroness. *Orishas,* or African gods and goddesses, were gradually melded over the centuries with Catholic saints. Sword-bearing Santa Barbara, for instance, became the representative for *Changó,* the *orisha* of violence. With his crutches and wounds, the humble and lame St. Lazarus, dressed in rags, represented the power of *Babaluaye,* the spirit that comforts and heals the sick.

In santería, the Virgin of Charity doubles as *OchDn,* or *Ochún,* a Yoruba goddess of eros and love. Beautiful, sexy and happy, she loves dancing, telling jokes and flirting. To keep or win a man, a woman can court *Ochún's* favour by putting five sweets smeared with honey in a bowl under her bed for five days; a man seeking love must chew cinnamon and drink honey.

Always dressed in yellow, the Virgin of Copper, as a mixed symbol of Christian charity and African sensuality, is celebrated by an annual festival on September 8. Pope Benedict XV declared her the patron saint of Cuba in 1916 following a petition from veterans of the War of Independence. Preserved in a glass case, the *Virgen del Cobre* wears a yellow satin, gold-encrusted dress and a replica of the coronation crown that was presented to her on her saint's day in 1936.

The virgin is a *mulatta,* a Black Mary, a symbol of the cross-fertilization of colours and beliefs. For anyone interested in Marian research, the cathedral is one of the most important sanctuaries for worship in the world. It was declared a *"basilica menor"* in 1977.

For hundreds of years Cubans have made offerings to the *Virgen del Cobre.* These are displayed behind the main altar at the Shrine of Miracles. The gifts include autographed baseballs, locks of baby hair, crutches, sporting trophies, a ship in a bottle, pictures of rafts that reached Florida, a golfball-sized gallstone, a television set, a Barbie doll, cooking oil, stuffed animals, a model Citroën, medals from Angola, a Mickey Mouse pendant, models of Jesus, clothing that belonged to revolutionary soldiers and even a poster asking for mercy for political prisoners.

Fidel Castro's mother, Lina Ruz, left a small statue of a golden guerrilla fighter at the church in the hopes of protecting her sons during the revolutionary campaign. Ernest Hemingway gave his 1954 Nobel Prize for Literature medal to the *Virgen del Cobre,* but a visitor smashed the glass display case in 1986 and ran off with it. Two days later Hemingway's medal was recovered by police; it's now kept in a vault.

Although the Virgin of Copper is 530 miles from Havana, millions of Cubans have made the pilgrimage to the Lourdes of Cuba. The *Virgen del Cobre* is also sometimes called the Virgin of the Mambises after the nineteenth-century independence fighters. The "Bronze Titan" Antonio Maceo, one of the most remarkable heroes of Cuba's War of Independence, paid tribute to the Virgin before taking up arms against Spain. Having asked for her protection, he is said to have survived hundreds of battles and 27 wounds.

Couples continue to come to Cuba's only basilica to give thanks to the Virgin for granting them a child. Others leave hand-written pleas for help. *"Virgen de la Caridad,"* reads one message on the wall, *"No me abandones."*

After Castro's revolution, Cubans surged to the shrine to give thanks for their deliverance from American imperialism and the dictatorship of Batista. The shrine has also been popular with Cubans seeking deliverance from Castro.

PIRACY, PIETY AND CRUELTY

In spite of the Virgin of Copper's protective presence, Henry Morgan and 900 pirates plundered nearby Santiago de Cuba with ease. The son of a well-to-do Welsh farmer, Morgan also undertook the first of three English raids on Havana. Now immortalized by a brand of rum, Captain Morgan was hired by Britain in 1668 to seek intelligence on Spanish activities. Operating under British licence from Port Royal in Jamaica, he ransacked Camaguey, pillaged the coast of Panama and retired comfortably to London.

Not to be outdone, a French buccaneer named L'Ollonois arrived in the Caribbean as an indentured servant. Under the employ of the French governor of Tortugas, L'Ollonois attacked the Cuban village of De Los Cayos and captured a Spanish frigate. He beheaded the surviving crew. Famous as a torturer, L'Ollonois was eventually captured by Nicaraguan Indians and dissected alive.

Profiteering was the dominant activity of the Caribbean and cruelty was an accepted practice. One major advantage that landowners had over pirates was that they could administer cruelty in the name of God.

In response to the Spanish Inquisition, a parish priest in Remedios decided that local inhabitants were possessed by devils. Some villagers were burned alive. Their homes were burned. Others were advised to move to land owned by the priest so that he could become their landlord.

The Count of Casa Bayona, feeling pious in the eighteenth century, invited 12 of his slaves to a feast on Holy Thursday. He personally washed each man's feet and promised a day of rest on Easter Sunday. Unfortunately this man's overseer didn't comply with this directive and the count's slaves rebelled in protest. Angered by the slaves' ingratitude, the count beheaded the 12 men whose feet he had washed. He left their heads on poles in the sugarcane fields to warn others.

Christ's teachings of resurrection led some Cuban slaves, particularly the Lucumi, to hope they could be reborn in Africa. To counteract the dangerous belief that slaves might escape to a better afterlife, their owners took to mutilating slaves' corpses.

The German naturalist Alexander von Humboldt was shocked by the callousness of the Spanish gentry in Cuba. "I have heard it discussed with the greatest coolness," he wrote, "whether it was better for the proprietor not to overwork his slaves, and consequently have to replace them with less frequency, or whether he should get all he could out of them in a few years and thus have to purchase newly imported Africans."

For the next hundred years aristocratic homes in Havana routinely had 20 to 30 slaves; wealthy homes could have as many as 100. Standard punishments were devised. The *novenario* was nine lashes a day for nine days; the *escalera* entailed tying a slave to a ladder prior to whipping. For the *boca abajo llevando cuenta*, a slave had to lie face down and count the lashes aloud; if he made a mistake in his counting the punishment recommenced.

In response to eighteenth-century slavery in general, the English poet William Cowper wrote "Pity for Poor Africans": "I own I am shocked at the purchase of slaves / And I fear those who buy them and sell them as knaves; / What I hear of their hardships, their tortures and groans, / Is almost enough to draw pity from stones. / I pity them greatly but I must be mum, / For how could we do without sugar and rum."

Cuban slaves had the legal right to buy their freedom and some mulattas were sought as mistresses, but the degradations suffered by blacks were endemic. Cirilo Villaverde's novel about a bewitching mulatta, *Cecilia Valdés,* written in exile in the 1880s, and Juan Francisco Manzano's *Poems by a Slave in the Island of Cuba,* an 1840 memoir of a slave who bought his freedom at age 38, are two of the rare literary depictions of everyday life for nineteenth-century slaves and blacks. In 1963, when he was 105, Estefan Montejo also published *Autobiography of a Runaway Slave.*

Slavery was not formally abolished in Cuba until 1888.

18TH-CENTURY COMMERCE AND ARISTOCRACY

The eighteenth century in Cuba was fraught with political, social and economic change.

Cuba was threatened by the French, the British and by pirates. As well, two black slave revolts, at a sugar mill west of Havana in 1727 and at the copper mine of Santiago del Prado in 1731, led to the creation of private militia to control labour.

Tobacco smoking and snuff taking were becoming fashionable crazes for the European aristocracy. After the Austrian

Hapsburgs lost the Spanish crown to the French Bourbons, the new rulers in Spain established a royal monopoly on Cuba's increasingly important tobacco trade, impoverishing many small farmers in the process. These farmers marched on Havana in protest.

In 1740 the *Real Compañía* was established to control all trade between Cuba and Spain, allowing Spanish investors to buy cheaply from Cuban producers. Farmers in eastern Cuba, as a result, were short of food and resources. They engaged in illegal trade to survive, sowing the seeds for more political alienation in the process.

Although the first sugar mills in Cuba had been built near Havana in the 1570s, cultivation of Cuban sugar had not been extensive in the sixteenth and seventeenth centuries because more efficient plantations had been established in Santo Domingo, controlled by the French, and in Jamaica, controlled by the English. As sugar production gradually increased in the 1700s, labour-intensive sugar plantations had long-term social effects on Cuban society.

Lacking European women, most Spanish overseers took black plantation slaves as their wives and mistresses. Unlike the English and French, the Spaniards were relatively liberal about accepting their mulatto offspring, thereby giving rise to some well-educated free citizens of mixed race. Some freed mulattas became fashionable mistresses in European and North American high society. Although slaves had the right to buy their freedom, they could not marry.

By 1760 Havana and Trinidad had developed a cosmopolitan elite, a "sugarocracy," with its own university in Havana, one that excluded mulattos, blacks, Jews and Moors. Havana was bigger than Boston or New York, but relatively undefended.

Slavery in Cuba was greatly boosted in 1762 when the English conqueror of Havana, George Keppel, third Earl of Albemarle, sold the 1,200 slaves he had used to take the city. To keep pace with the explosion of commerce under the British, more than 4,000 slaves were imported and sold in Havana during the 11-month British tenure. More than 40,000 slaves were imported to Cuba between 1763 and 1790. Many slaves from Africa were first brought to British islands, then transferred to Cuba.

With 200 warships and 20,000 men, the English under Lord Albemarle laid siege to Havana in 1762, first landing at Cojimar, then capturing Morro Castle. The short-lived English control of Havana had radical consequences. The Spanish trade regulations were removed for 11 months and an influx of foreign merchants created an economic boom. Trade with the British colonies in North America flourished as 700 merchant ships visited Havana.

The combined infusion of English capital and slave labour led to the creation of much larger sugar estates in Cuba, binding Cuba to an economy based on slavery.

The Seven Years' War ended in 1763 with the Peace of Paris. Cuba was returned to Spain; the English took control of Florida. The English agreed to rescind control of Cuba largely because influential English sugar planters in Jamaica didn't want Cuba to become a formidable rival for the English sugar market.

The new King of Spain, Charles III, emulated the liberal trade policies of the British and passed a commercial decree in 1764 to expand communication and trading with seven more Spanish cities other than Seville and Cadiz. More than 200 ships a year were encouraged to dock at Havana.

In the late 1700s Cuba began to trade directly with the independent 13 colonies of the United States, but the seeds of democracy were never part of the bargain. Whereas the U.S. Declaration of Independence was a revolutionary model throughout the West Indies, in the eighteenth century Cuba was no hotbed of romantic idealism.

The importance of sugar to Cuba increased with the 1791 slave revolt in neighbouring Santo Domingo under the black leader Francois Dominique Toussaint L'Ouverture, who died in prison in 1803. This bloody 10-year civil war, one that ultimately created the independent state of Haiti in 1805, helped the Cuban sugar industry in three important ways: With the rise of black independence in Haiti, Cuba's main competition in the Caribbean sugar market was decimated. French sugar planters were forced to flee to neighbouring Cuba, bringing with them improved production methods. The Cuban aristocracy recognized the importance of maintaining a tight rein on its slave labour, eschewing liberal tendencies.

In response to the Santo Domingo revolution, the amount of Cuban land devoted to sugar increased 16-fold over 30 years. By the end of the eighteenth century, sugar had indisputably eclipsed coffee as Cuba's main export.

By the first half of the nineteenth century, Cuban high society was extremely wealthy, decadent and reckless. Rogues rubbed elbows with the elite at cockfights; pampered women were cloistered like queens; house-building became intensely competitive; elaborate statues were erected; and the aristocracy craved entertainments and new fashions.

In the 1830s the pompish Governor Miguel Tacón y Rosíque sought to please Havana's opera lovers by striking a deal with the legendary smuggler Francisco Marty to build Teatro Tacón, at a cost of U.S. $2 million. The men first met when Marty agreed to be an informer on his fellow smugglers. Instead of accepting his monetary reward, Marty asked for a monopoly on fish sales. After Marty became exceedingly rich by building a new fish market, he struck a similar arrangement with Governor Tacón to build a new opera house. The ex-smuggler became a respected impresario by monopolizing opera in Havana, much to the dislike of the performers, who could not sing for anyone but Marty.

As the well-to-do sought new ways to spend their money, gambling, crime, romantic scandals and decadence made Havana, "the Paris of the Americas," into a risky outpost for cosmopolitans.

One year Havana's elite was enticed by a new type of delicacy called French sausage. Everyone agreed it was delectable. One day a "Habanera" sent her slave to the market to buy some. When her slave didn't return, the mistress angrily instructed authorities to find her runaway slave and punish her. The slave's head was found atop a pile of bodies at the "French sausage" factory, two miles outside the Monserrate gate. A gang of thugs had been capturing plump blacks for their mincer. Twelve were hanged, others were sent to work in Spanish mines, but the henchman bribed his way to freedom.

Law and order in nineteenth-century Cuba didn't always go hand in hand.

SEEDS OF REPUBLICANISM

Sugar barons ensured that notions of democracy and independence were viewed as dangerous. Although Cuba had its first newspaper as early as 1763 and a postal service, Cubans remained second-class citizens for their Spanish overseers, unable to prosecute a Spaniard or assume public office. By the close of the century, capitalism, colonialism, cruelty and racism had spread the seeds for rebellion.

During the first half of the nineteenth century there were numerous slave revolts, mostly minor. A rebellion in Camaguey was curtailed in 1805. Cuba's next Hatuey was a naive freemason named Ramón de la Luz who attempted to mount an uprising in 1809. That same year Joaquín Infante planned to overthrow the Spanish colonial government.

A free black carpenter in Havana named José Antonio Aponte, a self-styled Cuban Moses and the "Cuban Spartacus," organized a revolt by whites and blacks in 1811. As a devotee of santería, Aponte held political meetings in his home under the guise of holding ceremonies for *Changó,* Aponte's guiding spirit. He established connections with a black general in Haiti and created the Central Revolutionary Junta in Havana. Aponte and eight co-conspirators were hanged in 1812. Aponte's head was locked inside a cage in front of his home for public display.

One of the most advanced revolutionary organizations was *Los Soles y Rayos de Bolívar,* the Suns and Rays of (Simón) Bolívar, which proclaimed the creation of the Republic of Cubanacan in 1822. Led by José Francisco Lemus, this group called for the abolition of slavery. Most of the idealistic republicans were captured but some fled abroad, including José María Heredia, an influential poet, and Father Felix Varela, who published a pro-independence newspaper, *El Habanero,* from the United States.

Another uprising in Matanzas province in 1825 resulted in the deaths of 15 whites and 43 blacks. This led to more slave revolts on plantations. Insurrectionists were nearly always swiftly punished with torture, exile or death. Reprisals from Cuban authorities included being garrotted, hanged or drawn and quartered. "A thousand lashes were in many cases inflicted on a single negro," reported a visiting doctor. "A great number died under this continued torture, and still more from spasms, and gangrene of the wounds."

In 1827 Cuban exiles in Colombia and Mexico formed the Grand Legion of the Black Eagle, a secret society that spread to Cuba until it was uncovered in 1830.

More famously, a black female slave named Carlota, inspired by the successful revolt led by Toussaint, rebelled and died on November 5, 1843. Black Carlota would serve as a role model in 1975 when, on November 5, Cuba named its campaign to liberate Africans from imperialism in Angola "Operation Carlota."

AMERICAN IMPERIALISM

Encouraged by a doubling of territory after the Louisiana Purchase from France, expansionist U.S. President Thomas Jefferson sent General James Wilkinson to Cuba, asking if Spain wished to consider ceding Cuba for a price. Spain declined the offer.

"I candidly admit," wrote Thomas Jefferson in 1809, "that I have ever looked upon Cuba as the most interesting addition that can be made to our system of States." With Canada and Cuba as acquisitions, Jefferson imagined an invincible "empire of liberty."

By 1818 half of Cuba's trade was with the United States, and a royal decree opened Cuba to free trade.

By 1820 Cuba was the world's richest colony.

Whereas Mexico attained its independence from Spain in 1821 and Brazil broke with Portugal in 1822, Cuba remained tethered to Madrid. By 1835 Cuba and Puerto Rico were the only Spanish colonies yet to follow Simón Bolívar's stirring leadership and achieve independence from Spain.

By 1840 there were 436,000 slaves in Cuba, almost half the population. Although England had abolished its slave trade in

1808 and signed a treaty with Spain in 1817 to abolish the slave trade, slavery in Cuba persisted, legally and illegally, throughout most of the nineteenth century. In 1835 Spain and England signed another treaty that declared any ship carrying slaves could be seized. More than 1,000 ships a year still brought slaves into Havana.

Blacks were commonly sold by newspaper advertisements, alongside similar classified ads for horses. The Catholic Church did nothing to restrict the activities of Havana's thriving slave market.

By 1850 sugar accounted for 83 percent of Cuba's exports. A triangular shipping route evolved. Sugar was sent to the United States, rum was sent to Africa and slaves were sent to Cuba.

Cuban sugar planters approached the United States seeking closer economic or political ties, but when U.S. President James Buchanan repeatedly urged Congress to purchase Cuba, the issue of slavery blocked his ambition. (Presidents James Polk, Franklin Pierce, James Buchanan, Ulysses S. Grant and William McKinley all formally attempted to purchase Cuba from Spain. Polk offered Spain $100 million in 1848; Pierce offered $130 million in 1854; McKinley made the final offer of $300 million just prior to America's invasion in 1898.)

One way or another, in the words of U.S. Secretary of State William L. Marcy, Cuba was expected to "fall, necessarily, into the American continental system."

In 1850 600 soldiers set out from New Orleans, led by a former Spanish general named Narciso López, and captured the Cuban town of Cárdenas, near Mantanzas. López represented American interests that wanted to annex Cuba in order to preserve slavery. Forced to flee to Florida, López made a second Cuban landing several months later at Pinar del Rio, but was captured and executed by the Spanish. Ironically, the pro-American López designed the present Cuban flag with its single white star, derivative of the single star on the flag of pro-slavery Texas.

In 1853 the governor of Mississippi, General Quitman, accepted a proposal from *Junta Cubana,* a group of New York businessmen with Cuban ties, to invade Cuba for $1 million, declare a new republic and then, as Texas had done, accept annexation to the United States. Quitman planned to invade Cuba in February of 1854 but never did.

Most Cuban industrialists were greatly disappointed by Abraham Lincoln's Civil War victory in 1865, because it brought an end to the importation of new slaves to Cuba from the United States. To further protect their opulent living standards, sugar-plantation owners brought 120,000 Chinese labourers to Cuba in 1868 and also imported Mexican Indians to work as *macheteros,* labourers who cut sugarcane. Nonetheless, Lincoln's victory hastened the resolve of Cuba's sugar industry to become the most mechanized in the world. Latin America's first narrow-gauge railway, from the Guisnes sugar fields to Havana, had already been built in 1837.

The sugar barons imported the best products from Europe, where they frequently traveled, and they named their mansions with inspired one-word titles such as Confidence, Audacious and Hope. Some of Havana's streets were paved with granite from New England; the best architects were hired. One sugar planter in Trinidad built a fountain that spewed gin for men and eau-de-cologne for women. A sumptuous room was prepared for the king of Spain, kept ready at all times, should he ever wish to visit Havana. He never did.

Whereas other parts of Latin and South America were infused

with the inspirational philosophies and leadership of Simón Bolívar *(El Libertador)* and José de San Martín, the liberator of Argentina, Chile and Peru, Cuba remained staunchly conservative and was referred to in Madrid as "the Ever-Faithful Isle."

CARLOS MANUEL DE CÉSPEDES

The first leader to seriously challenge colonialism was a lawyer, poet and Oriente sugar planter named Carlos Manuel de Céspedes.

Born in Bayamo in 1819, he was educated at the University of Barcelona and at the Royal and Literary University of Havana. Céspedes had been banished to France for his political activities in Madrid, then imprisoned upon his return to Spain. He brought his radical sympathies to a meeting in Cuba held on August 4, 1868.

"Gentlemen, the hour is solemn and decisive," he said. "The power of Spain is

Carlos Manuel de Céspedes

decrepit and worm-eaten; if it still appears great and strong to us, it is because for more than three centuries we have contemplated it from our knees."

Céspedes sparked Cuba's first major attempt at revolution by freeing 30 slaves at *La Demajagua,* his family plantation near Manzanillo, on October 10, 1868. The following day, accompanied by 37 other planters, Céspedes arrived in the town of Yara, located west of Bayamo and east of Manzanillo, where they fought their first battle against the Spanish. In Yara he announced independence for Cuba in a manifesto, *Grito de Yara* (Shout of Yara).

Upon capturing the town of Bayamo, north of Santiago de Cuba, on October 20 with 147 men, Céspedes was joined by runaway slaves, known as *mambises,* as well as two free blacks, Antonio and José Maceo. The Spanish term *mambises* was derived from a Congolese word *mambi,* meaning despicable. One of Céspedes's rebels, a Bayamo lawyer named Perucho Figuerdo, composed the Bayamo anthem with the lyrics "To the battle, Bayames," which is now Cuba's national anthem.

The uprising was the start of the Ten Years' War between Spain and the Cuban rebels. Céspedes formed a small army to fight for independence from Spain and the gradual emancipation of slaves. First Cuban independence would be won; then Cuban slaveholders would be compensated for loss of manpower when slavery was abolished.

Antonio Maceo is Cuba's greatest military hero

The rebel troops were trained by General Máximo Gómez. Born in Santo Domingo in 1836, Gómez had initially supervised Spanish reserve troops when he arrived in Cuba in 1865. The other major figure to emerge from the Ten Years' War was Antonio Maceo. Born near Santiago de Cuba in 1848, Maceo was the son of a

Venezuelan mulatto and an Afro-American woman. He enlisted as a private in the rebel army in 1868; five years later he was promoted to the rank of general.

In 1869 the eastern rebels autonomously elected Céspedes as the first president of the Republic of Cuba. A Constituent Assembly prepared the new republic's rival constitution in Guaimaro.

The civil war continued for eight more years, resulting in the deaths of approximately 200,000 Cubans and 80,000 Spaniards. These included eight medical students from the University of Havana, executed by the government on November 27, 1871. These were the first of many Havana University students who became martyrs for the cause of Cuban independence. As well, Ignacio Agramonte led a revolt in Camaguey until he was killed in battle in 1873.

Céspedes was killed in an ambush at San Lorenzo in the Sierra Maestra in 1874. Having been unable to gain any direct support from a sympathetic U.S. President Ulysses Grant, most of Céspedes' revolutionaries reluctantly signed a peace accord offered by Spanish General Arsenio Martínez Campos in February of 1878.

A year later Spain announced a gradual abolition of slavery. It proved highly problematic. Ex-slaves would be required to continue working as "apprentices" for their owners until 1888. Some "employers" realized it was preferable to pay labourers only as they were required rather than to maintain workers as indentured employees. So the Ten Years' War wasn't finished.

Antonio Maceo and his troops opposed the accord signed with Havana because it didn't achieve either total abolition of slavery or independence. Rejecting amnesty offered by the pact signed in 1878, Maceo continued to fight against Martínez's troops for several months until he went into temporary exile in Jamaica.

José Martí, Cuba's
greatest patriot

Slavery officially became illegal in Cuba as of October 7, 1886, providing better-late-than-never freedom for the some 26,000 slaves that remained.

JOSÉ MARTÍ

To refer to José Martí as the George Washington of Cuba is to underestimate him as a poet and a statesman.

Born in Havana in 1853, José Martí was reared in Spain and returned to Cuba in his teens. He had six sisters and no brothers. His Spanish-born father, originally from Valencia, was a policeman in Havana; his mother was a Canary Islander. His main influence during his youth was a schoolteacher, Rafael María Mendive, a pro-independence romantic.

At 16 Martí started a newspaper, *La Patria Libre* (The Free Fatherland) and was soon convicted on a trumped-up charge of treason for writing a public letter that condemned a friend for attending a pro-Spanish rally. Martí began his six-year prison term with six months' hard labour in the San Lázaro stone quarry in Havana. His punishment left him physically impaired, partially blind and suffering from a hernia.

Awaiting exile to Spain, Martí spent nine weeks on the Island of Pines (now Island of Youth), off the southern coast, where Fidel Castro was later imprisoned for expressing similar views. Upon his deportation to Spain, Martí wrote *Political Imprisonment in Cuba* to depict the harsh treatment of his fellow inmates. For the remainder of his life, after his premature release and exile in 1871, Martí would wear a ring made from his shackles.

Martí earned a law degree by studying at the Central University of Madrid and at the University of Saragossa. He traveled extensively in Europe and also sent a political tract to the prime minister of Cuba arguing for Cuban independence. In 1875 he went to Mexico City, where he worked as a journalist; in 1877 he married the Cuban-born daughter of a wealthy Cuban sugar planter and taught in Guatemala.

The general amnesty in 1878 allowed Martí to return to Cuba. Prevented from practising law, he was soon known for his anti-colonial speeches. He organized support for rebel leaders Calixto García and Antonio Maceo after the outbreak of *La Guerra Chiquita* (the Little War). Arrested again in September, he was deported to Spain for the second time in 1879.

José Martí made his way to New York City in 1881 via Paris. Initially enamoured of American life, Martí came to view the U.S. as the greatest obstacle to Cuban independence. In the 1880s Martí understood that 83 percent of Cuban exports were going to the United States. Throughout the nineteenth century Cuba had more trade with the U.S. than with Spain. The island was becoming the third-largest trading partner for the U.S., after Britain and Germany. He feared most of all "the annexation of the peoples of our America by the turbulent and brutal North which despises them."

José Martí published several books and wrote many newspaper articles for *La Opinión Nacional* in Caracas and *La Nación* in Buenos Aires. While trying to unite all Cuban patriots and gaining an international reputation, he was not always on friendly terms with the black military leader Antonio Maceo and his leading military strategist Máximo Gómez. When both men arrived to discuss strategy, Gómez told Martí that Maceo ought to be in charge; there continued to be leadership tensions between the three men.

The older men were experienced on the battlefield; Martí had yet to prove himself as they had. This disparity, felt keenly by Martí, would later contribute to Martí's foolhardy bravado, resulting in his premature death, when he finally saw his first action in Cuba.

Not merely an intellectual, Martí formed the Cuban Revolutionary Party in 1892 after a decade of organizing among Cuban émigrés in the U.S., visiting cigar factories to find recruits for his cause. He drafted statutes for the CRP, reported on life in the United States for Latin American newspapers and rigorously dissected U.S. imperialism. Always formally dressed in a black suit, he was interviewed for the *New York Herald* prior to his invasion of Cuba. He said he looked forward to a "generous and brief war."

A liberal progressive, Martí consistently declared that sexual equality must be part of any doctrine for change in Cuba. Upon meeting Gómez in Santo Domingo, he had promised "a civilized war." He decreed that private property would be respected, civilians would be safe, and blacks could join his republican movement.

The Maceo brothers, Antonio and José, had landed in eastern Cuba from Costa Rica on March 31, 1895, and amassed an expeditionary force of 6,000 men. With only four companions, Martí and Máximo Gómez made a clandestine landing at Playa Imins on April 11, 1895, and united with the Maceo brothers. "He who wages war in a country that can avoid it is a criminal," Martí said. "So is he who fails to wage a war that cannot be avoided."

After 39 days in his homeland, José Martí supposedly went into battle armed only with a revolver and a collection of speeches by Cicero, carrying a picture of his daughter over his heart. In his youth he had prophesied that Cuba needed a generation of martyrs to liberate generations of slaves; he was determined to set an inspirational example.

José Martí, the poet and intellectual who coined the rallying cry *Victoria o el Sepulcro* (Victory or the Tomb), disobeyed orders from Máximo Gómez and headed away from safety towards the enemy. Conspicuously riding a white horse, he was shot and killed by three bullets on May 19, 1895, during his first day of battle at Dos Rios, on the Cauto River. This suicidal ride occurred east of Bayamo, where Céspedes had won his first major victory.

In his final letter José Martí had written that his duty was to create Cuba's independence and therefore prevent the United States from spreading over the West Indies. "All I have done up to now, and shall do hereafter, is to that end. I have lived within the monster and I know its entrails, and my sling is the sling of David."

José Martí remains most famous for his posthumous contribution to the lyrics of Cuba's best-known song, *Guajira gauntanamera,* or "Guantanamera" *(Yo soy un hombre sincero . . .).* It was composed by Joseíto Fernández in 1929. In the late 1950s musician Hector Angulo added some lyrics from Martí's *Versos Sencillos* (1891). During a concert at Carnegie Hall to express solidarity with Cuba in 1963, folksinger Pete Seeger sang the latter version. It was this Seeger rendition that became famous far beyond Cuba's shores.

Within and outside Cuba, the democratic spirit of Martí still kindles revolutionary fervour; for half a century his name has been invoked by both Castro and by anti-Castro forces. His books remain "bestsellers" in Cuba. *Sólo el amor engendra melodías,* he wrote. ("Only love makes melodies.")

Martí was as much concerned with the human soul as he was with political autonomy for his people. "It is a torment of man that to see well he must be wise. And then forget that he is wise." He was a leader with words, with deeds and with wisdom. "The desire to rise above oneself," he wrote, "is an unrelenting human longing."

SPAIN DEFEATED

With the death of Martí, the Revolutionary Army was undeterred. Under the direction of Máximo Gómez, the revolutionaries used *la tea* (the torch) as their most effective weapon. Rebels burned sugarcane plantations; factories and railways were also targeted. "It is necessary to burn the hive in order to disperse the swarm," Gómez said.

In January 1896 Gómez and his forces were approaching Havana; Antonio Maceo and his men had reached Pinar del Río

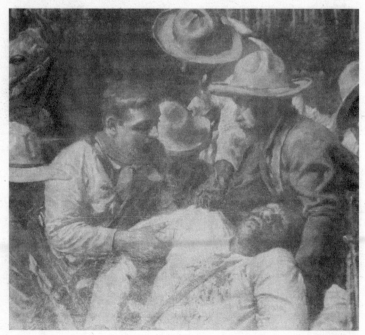

Antonio Maceo, the Bronze Titan, was finally killed in 1896

in the west. Mostly on horseback, Maceo's men had covered 1,000 miles in 92 days.

In retaliation, government troops executed *gaujiros* (country folk) who sympathized with Martí's call for freedom. Spanish General Valeriano Weyler, known as "the Butcher," arrived with 50,000 fresh troops and placed thousands of Cubans in resettlement (concentration) camps, where many died of disease and starvation. Weyler also responded with the *trocha,* a fortified ditch, to stop the advance of the rebels.

Weyler confronted the rebels in Pinar del Río. José Maceo was killed in battle at Loma del Gato on July 5, 1896; Antonio Maceo was captured and killed during the battle of Punta Brava in western Cuba on December 7, 1896, having responded to a request from Major General Máximo Gómez to unite their forces. The venerable Gómez, aged 75 by the time the war ended, died in Havana in 1905.

Covering the conflict as a *London Daily Graphic* war correspondent, Winston Churchill, at age 21, described accompanying Spanish troops as "awfully jolly." Sympathetically likening Spanish control of Cuba to England's control of Ireland, Churchill failed to grasp the nature of the struggle and saw it mainly in racist terms.

"A grave danger presents itself," Churchill wrote in the *Saturday Review.* "Two-fifths of the insurgents in the field are negroes. These men would, in the event of success, demand a predominant share in the government of the country, the result being, after years of fighting, another black republic."

Mark Twain was more forthright. When the U.S. intervened, he suggested the Stars and Stripes should be replaced by the Skull and Crossbones.

Territorially, Americans had eyed Cuba as a potential acquisition throughout the 1800s. President John Quincy Adams had prophesied Cuba would fall "like a ripening plum into the lap of the Union."

To "furnish the war," in the famous words of U.S. newspaper baron William Randolph Hearst, phoney stories were planted in Hearst's *Journal* about Cuban women being strip-searched by Spanish policemen aboard a U.S. ship. Hearst's cartoonist drew a suitably modest naked girl surrounded by men. The story headline was Does Our Flag Protect Women? Warmongers were further inflamed by a Hearst story that alleged a U.S. citizen might have been beaten to death in a Havana jail. Joseph Pulitzer's *World* was also a leading oracle for jingoism at the time.

More than two years after José Martí began the Second War of Independence in 1895, America sent the battleship USS *Maine* into Havana's harbour on a "peace mission" for a "friendly visit" on January 25, 1898. The United States entered the fray on the pretext of protecting U.S. citizens in Cuba. There were also substantial corporate and private American investments to be protected.

Equally relevant, America was ready to become a world power. Between 1884 and 1900, approximately three and a half million acres were added to the British Empire; it was time for Americans to take their share of the imperialist pie. A Democratic Senator named Mark Hanna said sending an American warship to Havana was "like waving a match in an oil well for fun." The wife of the *Maine's* executive officer similarly suggested "you might as well send a lighted candle on a visit to an open cask of gunpowder." The influential Henry Cabot Lodge had earlier remarked, "There may be an explosion any day in Cuba which would settle many things."

The USS *Maine* inexplicably exploded in Havana harbour, killing 266 American sailors on February 15, 1898. The captain and most of his officers were ashore at the time. Although the blast was probably accidental, and later attributed by some maritime experts to poor ship design, the newspapers of William Randolph Hearst and Joseph Pulitzer put the blame on the Spanish. The rallying cry for intervention was the slogan, "Remember the *Maine,* to hell with Spain."

Given the pretext of self-protection and retribution, President William McKinley argued on behalf of the "enforced pacification of Cuba." Eager to avoid further conflict, Spain declared a ceasefire in its war with the Cuban militants on April 9, but the Americans wanted a complete withdrawal of Spanish control.

In contravention of international law, McKinley instructed U.S. ships to proceed to Cuba's southeast coast and prepare to blockade the port of Santiago de Cuba. Two days later, on April 24, Spain responded with a formal declaration of war. The following day, the United States issued a formal declaration of war in return.

"If ever a war was misnamed," Theodore Draper has written, "it was the Spanish-American War. The name implies that only Spain and the United States fought in the war of 1898. It was not merely a Spanish-American war; it was also a Spanish-Cuban-American war and a Spanish-Philippine-American war. To leave out Cuba and the Philippines from the name of the war is to leave out the Cubans and Filipinos who were fighting Spain before the United States entered the war and without whom the United States would not have scored such an easy victory."

By May 28 the American fleet had gained control of Santiago de Cuba Bay, as instructed by McKinley. Whether Martí's co-revolutionaries wanted U.S. participation in their independence struggle was never of much concern to the Americans.

Contemptuous of Martí's ragtag rebel army and disconcerted to see that it mainly comprised blacks, a short-sighted military neophyte named Theodore Roosevelt led an inefficient but ultimately victorious charge by his "Rough Riders" at San Juan Hill, east of Santiago de Cuba, on July 1, 1898. With difficulty, his 6,000 American soldiers took most of a day to overcome 700 Spanish defenders. Thanks to exaggerations by the American press, Roosevelt, a future U.S. president, was touted as a hero.

Two days later the Spanish fleet tried in vain to circumvent the American ships in Santiago de Cuba Bay, with calamitous results. The mostly wooden ships caught fire easily and were run aground without a major fight. Regarded as the finest ship in the Spanish fleet, the 6,800-ton cruiser *El Christobal Colón* was beached and sank after a 50-mile chase. Only one American died; some 1,670 Spanish soldiers surrendered. Spain officially declared its defeat on July 17.

A victory march was staged through the streets of Santiago de Cuba. The Cuban freedom fighters, under the leadership of General Calixto García, weren't allowed into the city to participate. These *mambises* were ordered to surrender their weapons, but they didn't comply. García and his forces continued with the "mopping up" to the north, in Holguín and elsewhere, but the Cubans were not permitted to participate in the Spanish surrender of Havana that followed. The American flag was raised, not the Cuban flag.

Spain and the United States signed a bilateral armistice in Paris on December 12, 1898, giving the United States control of the Philippines, Guam and Puerto Rico. Cuba wasn't represented in these final negotiations.

That's how the twentieth century began in Cuba.

2 | AMERICAN CONTROL

Fulgencio Batista, the Pretty Mulatto

THE AMERICAN MILITARY RULED Cuba directly from 1899 to 1902, then again from 1906 to 1909.

The United States had agreed to withdraw troops only if Cuba would agree to remain as an American protectorate. By the turn of the century the United States had gained control of Puerto Rico, Guam, the Mariana Islands, the Philippines and the Hawaiian republic—and they were intent on realizing José Martí's worst fears in Cuba.

"It was the West—not Communist countries," American historian Henry Steele Commager has commented, "that invented imperialism and colonialism. We should remember that in the eyes of the nineteenth-century world it was the United States that was pre-eminently an expansionist and aggressive nation."

A BANANA REPUBLIC

The American military governor in Cuba, General Leonard Woolf, organized a constitutional convention in 1900 and presented a controversial amendment that was drafted by Republican Senator Orville Platt of Connecticut. Essentially it guaranteed the Americans the right to intervene in Cuba's domestic affairs. Cuba's first president, Tomás Estrada Palma, was forced to include the "Platt Amendment" in the Cuban constitution.

The Platt Amendment exacerbated Cuban resentment towards Americans, and its political repercussions would last for a century. In keeping with the constitutional proposal, Cubans were obliged to let the United States lease a naval base at Guantánamo Bay, in eastern Cuba, in perpetuity.

In 1901 U.S. General Woolf supervised a Cuban election. Women, Afro-Cubans and anyone with less than $250—a small fortune in Cuba—were not permitted to vote. "The people here," Leonard Woolf wrote to President McKinley, ". . . know they aren't ready for self-government. We are dealing with a race which has been steadily going down for a hundred years and into which we have got to infuse new life, new principles, and new methods of doing things."

The neo-Republic of Cuba was born on May 20, 1902, but under President Estrada it was an independent state in name only. The United States gained its Guantánamo Naval Base in 1903, the United Fruit Company purchased 200,000 coastal acres for $400,000, and by 1905 approximately one-quarter of Cuba was owned by Americans.

When Estrada resigned in 1906, after justified accusations of fraud during his re-election, the U.S. sent Marines to Cuba again, invoking the Platt Amendment, to re-establish military control from 1906 to 1908. During this period Cuba was initially ruled directly by Secretary of War William Howard Taft, then by a U.S. citizen appointee named Charles Magoon until January of 1909. Cubans, according to U.S. Senator Henry Cabot Lodge in a letter to President Theodore Roosevelt in 1906, "ought to be taken by the scruff of the neck and shaken until they behave themselves."

Incompetent and racist, Army General José Miguel Gómez served as president from 1909 to 1912, mostly lining his own pockets. None of José Martí's dreamed-of reforms were introduced. Corruption was rife, American control of Cuban resources was widespread, and the yoke of racism remained. In response to racism, Evaristo Estenoz, a veteran of the War of Independence, formed the Independent Coloured Party *(Agrupacion Independiente de Color)*. When this political organization was banned, Afro-Cubans rebelled against the new republic. During the so-called

Black Uprising of 1912, government forces, with the support of U.S. Marines, killed 3,000 mostly black Cubans.

Little had changed in Cuba for the ruling class or the ordinary people. Cuba had traded being controlled by Spain for being controlled by the United States.

"If we seize Cuba," slave owner Thomas Jefferson had said in 1817, "we will be masters of the Caribbean."

But Americans didn't have to annex Cuba politically to maintain power. It was diplomatically expedient and cheaper to manage Cuba with authoritarian domestic regimes that were closely overseen by emissaries of the various U.S. presidents. This model for imperialist control proved so successful in Cuba that it was repeated in Central American countries throughout the twentieth century.

In 1917 President Woodrow Wilson again sent U.S. troops to Cuba, this time to protect the regime of Conservative President Mario García Menocal (1912–1920) from Liberal Party opposition forces after his fraudulent re-election victory in 1916. "By a slight oversight," more votes were cast than there were voters.

Garcia Menocal proved understandably compliant to American wishes. He officially entered Cuba into World War I on April 7, 1917, the day after the United States had done so; he also opened up the island as a training base for U.S. Marines, who remained until 1922.

Having entered office with a fortune worth approximately $1 million in 1913, Garcia Menocal left office in 1921 with a fortune estimated at $40 million.

A succession of U.S.-supported *caudillos,* or strongmen, held power, including President Alfredo Zayas, whose administration cemented Cuban subservience by accepting a $50-million loan from J. P. Morgan & Company in 1923. This loan was orchestrated by General Enoch Crowder, an appointee of President Woodrow Wilson sent to Cuba in 1921 to supervise by-elections. A month after finalizing the J. P. Morgan deal, Crowder was named the first permanent U.S. ambassador to Cuba. In a reciprocal move, the first Cuban embassy was opened in Washington soon after.

In 1924 Cuban scholar Don Fernando Ortiz presented a paper called The Cuban Decadence. "In Cuba 53 percent of the population is illiterate; more than 50 percent of school-age children do not go to school; in the past 15 years illiteracy has risen 15 percent for young whites and 22 percent for young blacks; out of every 100 students, not one completes elementary school; the figure is one out of 215; and 20 percent of all political candidates nominated in 1922 had criminal records."

The most notable Cuban *caudillo* was General Gerardo Machado Morales, a convicted cattle rustler who operated a Havana theatre for pornography. Known as "the donkey with claws," Machado, a former butcher, had only three fingers on his left hand. An executive of the John Pierpoint Morgan financial empire, President Machado used police to brutally silence dissent during his reign of terror from 1925 to 1933.

When President Calvin Coolidge attended the 1927 Pan-American Conference in Havana, Coolidge described Cubans as "independent, free, prosperous, peaceful." Soon after Coolidge departed for Washington, Machado had four students accused of being communists thrown from the El Morro fortress in Santiago de Cuba into the sea with weights attached to them, to be eaten by sharks.

When Machado's term in office expired in 1928, he granted himself a six-year unelected extension with a new title— Illustrious and Exemplary Citizen. In the same year Irenée

Dupont bought hundreds of acres at Varadero Beach and built the opulent family mansion called Xanadu.

Resistance to Machado's police state increased dramatically in 1930 after the murder of Rafael Trejo, leader of the University Student Directorate. By the time Franklin Delano Roosevelt assumed the presidency of the United States, Cuba was a cauldron of corruption and unrest.

FDR's Assistant Secretary of State, Sumner Welles, went to Cuba as Ambassador Extraordinaire and Plenipotentiary, and he reported that Machado was a murderous liability. Unfortunately for FDR's administration, Machado was making so much money as president that he refused to leave the Capitolio.

At a cost of $17 million, Machado had erected a direct copy of the U.S. Capitol building as the centrepiece for his regime, located alongside the Gran Teatro de la Habana. The dome of the building soared 303 feet from the floor. In its cavernous entry hall Machado embedded an enormous 24-carat blue-white diamond that marked kilometre zero in Machado's highway connecting Havana to Santiago de Cuba. More astounding was the 49-ton statue of a woman, the embodiment of Cuba, which was built in Italy and delivered to Havana in three sections.

In 1933 a general strike and a military revolt finally prompted Machado to flee to the United States via Nassau with five revolvers and a fortune in gold.

Not all historians and political commentators have found the United States to be entirely blameworthy for its continued support of dictators and despots such as Machado in Latin America.

"Either the United States had to support corrupt governments in office," wrote Arnold Whitridge in 1961, "or permit revolutions that were bound to cause suffering to the population, financial depression, and eventually the establishment of another government, probably no less corrupt than the one it had supplanted. With some headshaking, the United States chose the first of these two unpleasant alternatives, knowing that whatever it did was sure to be wrong.

"If the United States is to blame for conditions in Cuba, it is for not having intervened more often, for having been too frightened of the stigma of imperialism."

Sumner Welles tried to install the son of Carlos Manuel de Céspedes as provisional president, but Céspedes Jr. was unpopular with both Cuban militia and students. Amid much political dissension and debate, the United States turned to a charismatic sergeant and stenographer, Fulgencio Batista y Zaldívar.

Batista was a sugar-field labourer's son from Oriente province. Born out of wedlock in 1901 and christened Rubén Batista, he was the son of a black woman; his paternal grandfather was an indentured Chinese labourer. As a young man in Oriente, Batista once worked for a landowner named Angel Castro, Fidel Castro's father.

Batista enlisted in the army, learned stenography and rose to the rank of sergeant. Initially viewed as a progressive and popular figure, Batista was affectionately known as the "pretty mulatto."

Batista had the support of students when he participated in a revolt of junior officers, the so-called "Sergeant's Revolt," to oust Céspedes Jr. after Céspedes had refused to make Batista chief of staff. For five days in September 1933, the puppet president was replaced with a junta of five, the *Pentarquía*—Dr. Ramón Grau San Martín, Sergio Carbó, Porfirio Franco, José Miguel Irisarri and Guillermo Portela.

Sumner Welles told Washington that the new junta was communistic. In response, America ordered 29 warships to Cuba and Key West and instructed American bombers to be ready. The junta appointed a liberal university professor, Dr. Ramón Grau San Martin, as Cuba's new president on September 10. The United States refused to recognize the new administration.

During his 100 days in office, Grau managed to realize some of José Martí's plans, but as soon as Grau started advocating an eight-hour day for workers, nationalization of utilities and agricultural land reform, he was seen as a danger by Washington. At the urging of the United States, Batista, self-promoted to colonel and chief of the army, overthrew President Grau on January 15, 1934.

Over the course of the next three days, Cuba had three more presidents. The United States approved the third candidate for the presidency, Colonel Carlos Mendieta Montefur, on the understanding that Batista would remain in the wings as an overseer. Batista's reputation as a strongman had been solidified after opposing army officers had holed up in the Nacional Hotel and threatened to fight; Batista shelled the hotel from land and sea until his adversaries surrendered.

In 1934, after a year of hectic meddling, the United States nullified the controversial Platt Amendment to save face internationally but modified its Guantánamo Naval Base lease in the process. As the oldest U.S. overseas military base, Guatánamo is a 44-square-mile reserve, 13 miles south of Guantánamo, that was originally leased on December 10, 1903. In 1934 the United States under Franklin D. Roosevelt modified the treaty to a 99-year lease to expire in 2033. Whereas Cuba was to receive $2,000 in gold coins as annual rent, this amount became $4,085 in 1934. (Fidel Castro cashed only the first lease payment he received while in power, refusing to cash further cheques, arguing the lease was not legitimate and promising to convert the luxurious American community into a hospital to serve all the Caribbean.)

Colonel Mendieta resigned after almost two years as president. During the brief administrations of three more Cuban presidents between 1935 and 1940, Cuban women gained the vote and Batista improved his connections with the U.S. Embassy. He also became a trusted ally of the American Mafia.

The profitable liaisons between Batista and the Mafia would have devastating effects on Cuban-American relations for the rest of the twentieth century.

BATISTA AND MOB RULE

During Prohibition, the Mafia used Cuba as a base for rum-running to the Florida Keys. New York bootleggers built rum factories in Cuba and made contracts with Cuban refineries to guarantee their steady supply of molasses. The facilitator for these dealings with Cuba was Meyer Lansky, "the Jewish god-father." When Prohibition ended in 1933, it was Lansky who surmised the Mafia had to diversify its interests. Gambling was Lansky's solution; heroin, prostitution and abortion were favoured by his associates.

Thanks to his direct associations with Batista, Meyer Lansky became the Mafia boss of Cuba. Lansky described Batista to Mafia boss Salvatore "Lucky" Luciano as "the best thing that ever happened to us. I've got him in my pocket, whether he's president or whether he puts some-body else in, no matter what happens.

Santos Trafficante Jr.

He belongs to us. I handle all his money—every dollar, every peso he takes. I'm handling the transfer of his account in Switzerland."

In the process of establishing his Cuban gambling syndicates, Lansky maintained links with Jack Ruby in Dallas and the Trafficante family in Tampa, Florida—a consortium that would be implicated in the assassination of President John F. Kennedy.

In 1938 Batista met with Meyer Lansky and invited him to take control of Havana's racetrack casino at Oriental Park and the Casino Nacional in Marianao. Ironically, these operations were renowned for being fixed; Batista was asking the American Mafia to clean them up.

"In the kingdom of the blind," Santos Trafficante Jr. later observed, "the blind man is king."

Knowing that high rollers would not risk money in casinos that were obviously crooked, Meyer Lansky brought in his own croupiers and pit bosses. With kickbacks to Batista, the Mafia operations in Cuba flourished as the reputations of Havana's casinos improved, attracting respectable clientele and some big-name entertainers until the onset of World War II. Although tourist revenues plummeted during the war, sugar prices skyrocketed and Cuba's economy was relatively secure.

Spurred by the success of his new gambling interests, Batista ran for president in 1940, defeating his old rival, Ramón Grau San Martin. He remained in office until 1944, the year President Roosevelt reportedly used Meyer Lansky to send a message to Batista, asking him to resign in favour of free elections. Surprisingly, Batista's candidate lost to Grau and Fulgencio Batista "retired" to Daytona Beach, not far from Lanksy's Florida headquarters, having reportedly accumulated $20 million.

After the war American tourists began to return in large numbers to Havana. The sun and sand and bordellos also provided the perfect backdrop for the most important meeting of Mafia bosses to be held since the Depression.

In December of 1946 Frank Sinatra was flown to Havana, accompanied by two of Al Capone's cousins, to perform for America's top mobsters and Meyer Lansky's guest of honour, "Lucky" Luciano. Sinatra brought with him a gold cigarette case for presentation to Luciano at his Christmas Eve concert. Having been deported from the U.S. and forced to live in Rome, Luciano had acquired a false passport. The "Boss of Bosses" rejoined his old cohort Lansky in the October prior to the December 22 meeting to make their plans.

In attendance at the elegant Hotel Nacional summit were Mafiosi Frank Costello, Tommy Lucchese, Vito Genovese, Moe Dalitz, Joe "Bananas" Bonanno, Joe Adonis, Albert Anastasia, Tony Accardo, Carlo Marcello, "Dandy Phil" Kastel and Santos Trafficante Jr.

Not in attendance was Bugsy Siegel, who was in Las Vegas building the Flamingo Hotel and reputedly skimming Mafia funds from the construction project. At the Havana summit Lansky and Luciano reluctantly agreed their childhood friend, Siegel, had to be killed. They couldn't tolerate a thief. Siegel's life was spared on Boxing Day when they learned Siegel's Flamingo opening was a bust.

Lucky Luciano had big plans. For gambling, he wanted to convert the Island of Pines into the new Monte Carlo. In terms of drugs, the Mafia envisioned that Cuba could serve as the ideal transitional point for shipping drugs into the United States from his sources in Europe, or from new sources in South America.

After the meeting, the flamboyant Luciano, who was often seen around the city in the company of beautiful women, was tracked by U.S. federal narcotics agents to the Havana racetrack. Orders came to Havana from Washington, D.C., that the highly conspicuous Luciano would have to return to Italy. In 1947 Meyer Lansky was left in control of their shared plans.

As the Mafia feared, voters in Florida declined to legalize gambling. The police closed Meyer Lanksy's operations in Miami, and the Kefauver Crime Commission in the U.S. attempted a national crackdown. In response, to instigate the Mafia's back-up plan for mobilizing their resources, Lansky paid Fulgencio Batista a visit at his Daytona Beach home. He asked Batista to return to Cuba, as president, and clear the way for major gambling initiatives. Batista promised to oblige.

Mafia resources stifled in the U.S. would be transferred to Cuba. It was a relatively simple matter of telling Cuban President Carlos Prío Socarras, elected in 1948, to step aside. Meyer Lanksy himself delivered a $250,000 bribe, while making Prío an offer he couldn't refuse. Fulgencio Batista returned to power in Cuba on March 10, 1952, in a coup that was unopposed.

On March 10, 1952, General Batista suspended Cuba's constitution, cancelled elections and became Cuba's dictator. The U.S. administration of Harry Truman recognized Batista's regime almost immediately and sent economic and military aid. Four months later Cuba formally became a member of the Organization of American States (OAS).

Once again, Meyer Lansky took pains to clean up the notoriously crooked Havana casinos. He began with the Montmartre Club, then installed his brother Jake as the pit boss at the Hotel Nacional, an operation he shared with the Cleveland syndicate headed by Moe Dalitz. Meyer Lanksy's main collaborator in the expansion of Mafia operations was Santos Trafficante Jr., who controlled gambling at the San Souci nightclub and casinos in the Sevilla-Biltmore, Capri, Comodoro and Deauville Hotels. Cuban-Italian Amieto Batistti controlled heroin and cocaine links with the U.S.

For Americans, Havana was Babylon. Or as Irving Berlin coyly sang about Havana, "Dark-eyed Stellas light their feller's panatelas." Promiscuity was rampant. Cocaine was provided for gamblers who didn't want to sleep. Marijuana was easily procured. Prostitution was so endemic that businessmen arriving at the airport could select their mulatta beauties in advance from photographs.

Live sex acts were common. The most famous performer for *los exhibiciones* at the Shanghai Theatre was Superman, also available for private showings with female partners. The upper-class Casa Marina was known as a source of teenage boys and girls, available for sex, with a surcharge for virgins. Lesbian sex could be viewed at the Blue Moon. Havana had approximately 2,000 prostitutes. Each brothel had to pay uniformed police officers in order to remain in business.

Hotel revenues were tax-free. Personal cheques from gamblers were flown to Miami on a daily basis to clear the bank. A new airline was started. Batista creamed millions from huge construction projects, including a phoney plan to dig a canal across Cuba, beyond his enormous share in gambling operations. Lansky had to found two banks in Florida just to launder his Cuban profits. The two men maintained a brotherly compact, accumulating untold millions in Swiss bank accounts.

The decadence engendered by the Batista/Lansky alliance was titillating to Americans, who didn't require any visas to enter

Cuba. Maurice Chevalier, Nat King Cole and America's top jazz bands all contributed to the rum-soaked, carnal atmosphere. Errol Flynn liked to visit Havana in his yacht. Movie star George Raft, who portrayed gangsters in Hollywood films, was the tough-guy emcee at the Capri's Red Room. When Lansky opened his Internacional Club casino, his headline act was Eartha Kitt. When Lansky opened his most ambitious project, the 383-room Hotel Riviera, the headline entertainer at the Copa Room was Ginger Rogers.

Havana was so out of control that the mayor reportedly killed himself in despair in 1947.

In 1957 one of the many dignitaries who came to Havana was Senator John F. Kennedy of Massachusetts. According to Trafficante Jr., John F. Kennedy was his guest at the Hotel Commodoro when three prostitutes were provided at once. Mafia lawyer Frank Ragano recounts in his 1994 autobiography, *Mob Lawyer,* that Trafficante and his casino partner Everisto Garcia proceeded to watch JFK's sport through a two-way mirror. While there is no proof of this allegation, it is tempting to assume Trafficante's alleged voyeurism would have been filtered back to the Kennedy administration during his presidency, possibly even affecting some of Kennedy's decisions regarding both the Mafia and Cuba.

CIA director Allen Dulles, a former president of the United Fruit Company, visited Havana in April of 1955. He successfully urged Batista to open a police intelligence bureau, funded and overseen by the CIA, called the Buro de Represion a las Activides Communistas (BRAC). Dulles's brother was John Foster Dulles, the U.S. secretary of state, long-time legal counsel for, and investor in, the United Fruit Company (later United Brands and Chiquita Brands). Walter Bedell Smith, who headed the CIA prior to Dulles, became president of the United Fruit Company after the CIA overthrew the democratically elected government of Jacobo Arbenz in Guatemala during "Operation Success" in 1954.

Richard Nixon also visited Havana, once as a senator and once as Eisenhower's vice-president. In the latter capacity, the future president of the United States and his wife were photographed at a lavish rooftop party with Batista and his Mafia friends at the Sevilla-Biltmore Hotel, overlooking Havana, in January of 1955. Standing unopposed, Batista had won presidential elections in November of 1954; Nixon's congratulatory visit conferred the blessings of the United States. Richard Nixon later likened Fulgencio Batista to Abraham Lincoln.

(After the Revolution, Batista would live unmolested in Spain. He was one of the world's richest men until his death in 1973.)

Conversely, for Cubans, under the administration of President Batista and his notorious police chief, Captain Ventura, Cuba was a police state. While the elite enjoyed the high life in Havana, ordinary Cubans were starving in shanty-towns. A quarter of Cuba's population was unemployed. Few had running water. Most were barely literate. "In the eyes of the United States," wrote Graham Greene, author of *Our Man in Havana,* "government terror was not terror unless it came from the left."

While Batista concentrated on profiteering in Havana, Cuba's rural economy was precariously dependent on one crop, sugar, primarily controlled by American companies. Even though Cuba became the world's leading producer and exporter of sugar in the 1950s, after the war, when Cuba was producing five million tons of sugar a year, Cuba's production would have had to double to create a balance of trade with the U.S.

This was the socio-political climate that engendered the nationalism of a brash young student leader and lawyer named Fidel Castro.

CASTRO'S EARLY LIFE

Fidel Alejandro Castro Ruz was born out of wedlock during a cyclone, on August 13, 1926, at approximately 2 a.m., at a remote *hacienda* called Manacas, at Birán. Born on the thirteenth, 13 being half of 26, Fidel Castro later favoured the number 26 for major decisions and announcements.

The rough-hewn Castro home was located southwest of Mayari, near the northeast coast of Cuba, formerly a part of Oriente province. Birán didn't have a church. The Castro family owned the store, the barn, the bakery and the small slaughter-house. There was also a small school and a post office.

The Castro house was built on stilts, in the style of Galician architecture. Domestic animals, including cows, were kept under the house prior to the building of a barn. Housekeeping was minimal. Chickens roosted on the chairs. During the sugar harvest, cockfights were held every Sunday. Only 60 miles away, an Americanized bourgeoisie—also dependent on the United Fruit Company—resided in Banes, on the coast, where Fidel Castro would court his only wife, the daughter of Banes's mayor.

Fidel Castro's father, Angel Castro, had been born in the northern Spanish province of Galicia on December 8, 1875. At the age of 20, as a poor "Gallego" in a barren, mountainous region, he reportedly accepted payment from a rich family to go to Cuba and fight in place of their son.

Fighting on the losing side of the Spanish-American War, Angel Castro developed his enduring grudge against the United

Off-limits to tourists, here is where Fidel Castro was born during a cyclone
on August 13, 1926

States. He returned briefly to Galicia but decided his prospects
were better in eastern Cuba.

At first, he worked as a day labourer for United Fruit, the
American company that owned the sugar mills and leased most
of the land. He became a sugarcane contractor, then eventually a
wealthy landowner. His inland farm was so remote that Angel
Castro didn't pay taxes in his early years of operation. As a landlord, he gained influence in local politics and became accepted by
the gentry.

Angel Castro first married a "respectable" schoolteacher named
María Louisa Argote. She bore him two children, Pedro Emilio and
Lidia. This first marriage disintegrated after Angel Castro began to
have sexual relations with a new teenage housemaid, Lina Ruz
González, who was hired when she was approximately 14.

Angel Castro granted his first wife only a small pension; their
oldest daughter, Lidia, was sent to live with her mother, whereas

their son, Pedro Emilio, remained on the farm with his father. Resentful of her banishment from her father's home, Lidia became known as Perfidia but became a staunch supporter of her half-brother Fidel.

Fidel Castro's mother, Lina Ruz González, had come to Oriente when her father had driven an ox cart 600 miles from Pinar del Rio province.

"My mother was practically illiterate," says Castro. "She learned how to read and write all by herself." A fervent Catholic and also a santería spiritualist, she prayed every day and lighted candles to the *Virgen del Cobre*. (Castro's mother and her mother would pray and make many vows on behalf of Fidel Castro, but after he allowed the family farm to be attacked during the revolution, she turned against him. She died on August 6, 1963, estranged from him, and was buried at Manacas, alongside the grave of Angel Castro.)

Fidel Castro was the second child of his father's second family. His sisters from the second family were Angelita, Juanita, Emma and Agustina; his older brother was Ramón; his younger brother was Raúl. "Despite their colourful life together," writes anti-Castro biographer Georgia Anne Geyer, "they had no sense of family."

At Manacas Fidel Castro developed his habit of eating while standing. Family manners were minimal. His mother rode around the plantation with a pistol and a Winchester, wearing boots and firing in the air to call the family to meals. The only "legitimate" son, Castro's older half-brother, Pedro Emilio, initially received preferential treatment from his father. Pedro Emilio later portrayed the family's lack of harmony in a radio soap opera, *The Castros of Birán,* until he was persuaded, probably with a bribe from his father, to discontinue it.

Reports on the size of the Castro ranch and sugarcane plantation vary. Castro estimates his father owned about 2,000 acres
and leased nearly 2,500. For labour, there were approximately
300 families totalling 1,000 people. Most of the workers were
very poor Haitians.

"All of the children went barefoot," Castro recalls. "They were
my friends and comrades in everything. We went to the river, the
woods and the fields together to hunt and to play. During my
vacations, they were my friends and my buddies. I didn't belong
to another social class. We were always together and had all kinds
of relationships. I had a very free life there. There was no bourgeois or feudal society in Birán." But Castro has conversely said,
"Everyone lavished attention on me, flattered, and treated me
differently from the other boys we played with when we were
children. These other children went barefoot while we wore
shoes."

At age five Fidel Castro was sent to Santiago de Cuba with his
older brother and sister for schooling. It was a difficult year in
which they often went hungry, simply because they had been
placed in custodial care.

Because he hadn't been baptized, Fidel was sometimes called a
Jew, a derogatory term he didn't fully understand. His religious
instruction had been minimal in Birán because the priest had
only visited once a year. Later he would also be teased for his lack
of an aristocratic background.

Castro's agnosticism didn't preclude his having an interest in
the Bible and spirituality. During the revolution he sometimes
wore a small medallion of the Virgin of Copper that was sent to
him by a young girl in Santiago de Cuba—not given to him by
his mother as is generally believed—but he never considered
himself to be formally religious. (The Communist Party of Cuba

specified that members of any organized religion could not be members of the party.)

In Santiago de Cuba Castro was finally baptized after the sister of his teacher married the Haitian consul. This Haitian consul became Fidel Castro's godfather. Castro's father wanted an extremely wealthy man named Don Fidel Pino Santos to be the godfather, hence the name Fidel. "They could wait six years to baptize me, but they couldn't wait six years to give me a name. And that is the origin of my name. I actually owe it to a very rich man."

At age seven he staged one of his first rebellions, misbehaving in the hope that he would be sent to a different school. It worked. He spent the next four years at La Salle School in Santiago de Cuba.

In the fifth grade he transferred to a more prestigious Jesuit school, *Colegio de Dolores* (School of Our Lady of Sorrows), where he developed his own values and became critical of cruelty and prejudice. "There weren't any black students at the Colegio de Dolores; all were supposedly white. This puzzled me several times."

Not yet a teenager, he wrote a letter to President Franklin D. Roosevelt. "If you like, give me a ten dollar bill green american, in the letter, because never, I have not seen a ten dollars bill green american and I would like to have one of them." The president of the United States thanked and congratulated him for his letter but he did not enclose ten dollars.

At age 10 or 11 he attended summer-school tutorials given to his sister as she was preparing for high school. The teacher was a black woman named Professor Danger. "She was the first person I ever met who encouraged me; who set a goal, an objective, for me."

Argumentative at home and at school, Fidel Castro organized a protest against his father when he was 13 and later criticized his father's business dealings. Fidel became known for his volatile temper and his fiercely competitive behaviour. Many years later his friend Gabriel Garcia Márquez wrote, "I do not think anyone in this world could be a worse loser."

At the boarding schools in Santiago, even though he excelled academically and athletically, he was taunted for his background. He was also taught that to be a Protestant, a Jew, Muslim, Hindu or Buddhist, Animist or a participant in any other religion was a sin worthy of severe punishment. Although something of a dandy, Castro refused to conform to bourgeois manners or elitist distinctions.

"I consciously decided to seek new horizons," he says. On his own, he decided to transfer to the top Jesuit school in the country, the *Colegio de Belén*. At age 16, arriving in Havana for the first time, he enrolled with the cream of the Cuban aristocracy. "He was a boy both rough and charming," recalls his mentor Father Armando Llorente, "a mixture of Spain and Cuba."

His abilities at basketball later earned him the athlete of the year award, but he had to work very hard to excel. He practiced so hard that the priests had to install a light on the basketball court so he could practice at night, earning himself the nickname *El Loco Fidel*. "If I hadn't been an athlete," he says, "I wouldn't have been a guerrilla." Castro was also an avid mountaineer and played baseball.

The story is often told that Fidel Castro once received a tryout from a scout associated with the Washington Senators. He is circumspect and mentions he talked with the scout who recruited Cuban players. By Castro's own admission, he wasn't

A Cuban postcard: "If I hadn't been an athlete, I wouldn't have been a guerrilla," said Fidel Castro

major league material. It is nonetheless often said that if Fidel Castro had only had a better curveball, the Cuban revolution might have never happened.

"Instead of becoming a Senator," says Tommy Lasorda, who met Castro, "he became a dictator."

Although assertive and athletic, he did not like to dance or sing. Politically, Castro was interested in Hitler, Mussolini and the Spanish Falangist José Antonio Primo de Rivera. The latter founded the Spanish Fascist Party and was a proponent of *Hispanidad,* a movement that called for the unity of Spanish-speaking people around the world.

Most of the other students and staff at Belén College were wealthy and conservative; he had to prove that he was equal to them or better. To prove his mettle as someone willing to do things others wouldn't dare, he once bet another student that he could ride a bicycle into a stone wall. He rode down a large hall with columns and crashed into a column, injuring himself.

"More than once, in some of those schools for the wealthy and privileged, among whom I found myself, it occurred to me to ask why there were no black children there," he said. "I have never been able to forget the totally unpersuasive responses I received."

Castro entered University of Havana law school in 1945, having received a new American car from his father as a present. He later regretted his legal studies, saying he should have studied something more practical, but for such an argumentative person it was a logical path.

During his university days, Cuba's government was unstable. The Havana campus, where police were not allowed, was rife with student violence and confrontations. Violent gangs called *bonches,* or bunches, were fearsome. Upon his arrival, Castro was nicknamed "Greaseball" and made a name for himself by challenging the president of the Student Federation. His years at university, he later said, were "much more dangerous than all the time I fought against Batista from the Sierra Maestra."

It was not uncommon for menacing political gangs to cruise through the streets in large American cars, carrying machine guns and threatening the professors. Castro adapted to this atmosphere of fiery rhetoric and hooliganism without hesitation, instigating protests, watching films of Mussolini to hone his public-speaking skills, and carrying a gun.

His younger brother, Raúl, also attended the University of Havana. Much more so than Fidel, Raúl developed a strong interest in Marxist/Leninist theories. Whereas Fidel was primarily concerned with the acquisition of power, his brother was more genuinely curious about the ideal form that political power might take. He joined the youth wing of the Communist Party and helped edit *Saeta,* its publication. In 1953 he attended the World Communist Youth Festival in Sofia, Bulgaria.

Fidel Castro appeared on the front page of a Havana newspaper in 1946. The students were protesting higher bus fares, directly criticizing President Ramón Grau San Martín. Injured during a protest rally, Castro and three other student leaders met with President Grau to discuss the situation. During that meeting Castro envisioned taking power by throwing the president off the balcony.

He became increasingly active in formal political groups, joining the Revolutionary Insurrectional Union, but he was never trusted enough or liked enough to gain leadership. He wanted to become president of the Federation of University Students. When his father learned about his passion for politics, he rescinded his $500-a-month support. Frustrated, in December Fidel Castro participated in an assassination attempt on a rival student leader, Leonel Gómez.

In 1947 he became a founding member of the Cuban People's Party (the Ortodoxos) and he temporarily discontinued his law classes. He also participated in a military training program on a remote Cuban key called Cayo Confites with 1,200 Cubans, Dominicans, Venezuelans and Costa Ricans under Dominican patriot Juan Bosch. This international force hoped to invade the Dominican Republic and overthrow the dictatorship of Rafael Trujillo.

Castro's father and mother both summoned him to Havana to protest his participation in the Cayo Confites Expedition. He refused to listen. The non-secretive Expedition predictably fell apart after President Grau ordered them back to Cuba; Castro supposedly had to swim to shore in shark-infested water to escape from his political rivals within the Cayo Confites Expedition itself.

There were 14 newspapers in Havana; Fidel Castro began to use them to his advantage. In 1947 he accompanied the historic, 300-pound *La Demajagua* bell from Céspedes's plantation in Manzanillo to Havana. With fanfare, Castro brought the bell to the Gallery of Martyrs at the university to be pealed during an anti-government demonstration. He did so after President Grau had requested permission from the city fathers of Manzanillo to use the historic bell in Havana for his celebrations and he had been refused.

As Gabriel Garcia Márquez has suggested, Fidel Castro's sense of one-upmanship has long bordered on the pathological. A Cuban doctor who formerly supported him, Dr. Mariano Sorí Marín, once described him as "a megalomaniac with a sense of grandiosity."

In March 1948 at age 21, Castro and three other Cubans arrived in Bogotá, Colombia, to express their solidarity with other anti-imperialist Latin American students during the Ninth International Conference of American States. Argentinian dictator Juan Perón paid for their transporta-

Gabriel Garcia Márquez on Fidel: "I do not think anyone in this world could be a worse loser"

tion. Students went to Colombia to protest a summit meeting of hemispheric foreign ministers, under U.S. auspices, to lay the foundation for the Organization of American States.

Castro was one of the students who showered anti-American leaflets from the balcony of the assembly. He was taken to a police station, warned about his behaviour, but he was not arrested. On April 7 he and Rafael del Pino met with Colombian Liberal leader Jorge Aliecer Gaitán. Tragedy struck on April 9 when a mestizo Colombian named Juan Roa assassinated Gaitán. Fidel Castro had been on his way to a second meeting with Gaitán when the assassin struck.

Three days of bloody rioting ensued. Estimates of how many people were killed vary from 3,000 to 5,000. Castro took up arms during the demonstration but escaped arrest by taking refuge in the Argentinian embassy. He was flown back to Cuba in a cargo plane that was taking prize bulls to Havana for a bullfight.

Castro's experiences in Colombia provided an important bond with Ernesto "Che" Guevara, who would visit Colombia in 1952. "Of all the countries we have traveled through," Guevara wrote, "this is the one in which individual guarantees are the most suppressed; the police patrol the streets with their rifles on their shoulders and constantly demand one's passport . . . and the memory of the 9th of April 1948 weighs like lead over everyone's spirit." Years later when Guevara decided to leave Cuba to foment revolution in Colombia and Bolivia, Fidel Castro understood and approved.

Incongruously, on October 10, 1948, the same year he'd traveled to Colombia, Fidel Castro married a wealthy and vibrant philosophy student, Myrta Díaz-Balart. Her father was mayor of Banes and a lawyer for Batista. Although Castro was a very close friend of Myrta's brother, Rafael Díaz-Balart, her family wasn't pleased.

The couple received $10,000 from Myrta's father for a three-month honeymoon and also accepted $1,000 spending money from Fulgencio Batista. Following in the steps of his hero, José Martí, Castro made his first trip to New York, partially subsidized by the man he would replace. He lived the high life and was surprised to find copies of *Das Kapital* openly for sale in bookshops. He bought one.

In New York Castro spent some of their $10,000 for a white Lincoln Continental with push-button controls. His brother-in-law Rafael later noted, "He only had the money to buy a new car, like a Pontiac, but Fidel fell in love with his enormous Lincoln, it was *grandissimo*."

The friendship between the pro-democracy Rafael and Fidel soured when Fidel did not properly care for his wife and son and exhibited extremely violent tendencies. Once, driving in a car to a meeting with Rafael and Rolando Amador, Fidel stopped the car and started shooting at cows. "When I asked him why," Rafael recalled, "he said he was practising. That was how easily he could later shoot informers."

The couple's son, Fidelito, was born in 1949. During the boy's extremely chaotic upbringing, his mother was often without enough money to pay for electricity and food.

"Fidel never knew how to love," said the poet Jorge Valls. "Giving himself was something he didn't know. He was too worried about his theatrical role."

Years later Fidelito was kidnapped on behalf of Fidel Castro in Mexico City, then re-kidnapped by his mother.

(Cuban family law affords strong paternal rights. As Fidel Castro's only legitimate son, Fidelito was eventually educated in Russia, married a blond Russian and had three children. He became more widely known to the Cuban public as Castro's atomic energy director, coordinating a truncated nuclear power plant project in Cienfuegos. Speculation emerged in the 1980s that the hot-tempered Fidelito might be groomed as his father's successor, instead of Raúl. In spite of Fidel Castro's ongoing affairs and flirtations with other women, Fidel and Myrta were not divorced until 1954. The boy's mother left for the United States, remarried and moved to Spain. Living in a Madrid apartment building, she saw their son occasionally during Fidelito's visits to European capitals.)

Carlos Prío Socarrás had become president and "General" Batista had been elected senator for Las Villas province while running his campaign from Florida. When an American soldier was seen urinating on the José Martí statue in Parque Central, Fidel Castro galvanized a demonstration against the drunken American soldiers. Cuban patriots were beaten back by police outside the American embassy.

After obtaining his law degree from the University of Havana in 1950, Fidel Castro seldom took cases. Perhaps his most famous case arose in 1952 after Castro wrote a series of articles in the *Alerta* newspaper protesting the use of forced military labour on private estates. He then supplied data and photographs to the courts to support his case. He used the opportunity to garner military favour by arguing for an increase in army salaries.

Similarly, Castro supplied photos of President Carlos Prío's estate 12 miles from Havana to prove the links between the president and some lawless *pistoleros*. By posing as a gardener, Castro was able to supply *Alerta* with pictures of the president's extravagant mansion accompanied by the headline "This is the way the President lives with the money he has robbed from the people."

Although he opened an Havana office at Tejadillo 57, near the docks, under the name Azpiazu, Castro y Rosende, he preferred not to work. Instead he continued to rely upon an allowance from his father. Angel Castro disapproved of his son's political hooliganism, but he continued to finance some of his legal political gambits. Angel died before his son's invasion of Cuba, on October 21, 1956, and was buried at the (off-limits) family farm in Birán.

In 1951 Castro's brother-in-law, Rafael, obligingly arranged for Castro to meet with Batista at his *finca*. Batista later remarked to Rafael, "Your friend is very intelligent, but dangerous."

That same year both Raúl and Fidel Castro spoke out against the Prío government's intention to send Cuban soldiers in support of the American offensive in Korea. Whereas his brother was an advocate of communism, Fidel Castro preferred to quote from the socially acceptable works of Cuban patriot José Martí. On the surface, with a socially acceptable wife and some bourgeois relations, Fidel Castro could appear "orthodox" when necessary or prudent. Hence Fidel Castro was accepted as a candidate for the Ortodoxo Party, a liberal party founded by Senator Eduardo "Eddy" Chibás.

Chibás was a plantation owner's son who had been a member of the venerable student organization, the Directorio Estudiantil Universitario (DEU). Founded in response to Machado's dictatorship, the DEU had a military wing that made bombs, killed the president of Machado's Senate, his henchmen and eventually Machado himself.

Chibás became the great hope of Cuba in early 1951 largely on the strength of his radio

Eddy Chibás became the great hope of Cuba in 1951 on the strength of his radio speeches

speeches. His popularity was at its height when, at age 43, he shot himself in the stomach with a revolver at the end of a passionate radio address. Supposedly he was distraught because he had made an allegation of corruption that he was unable to prove. Unfortunately this dramatic suicide occurred during a commercial break. Chibás didn't realize the allotment of airtime he'd purchased had expired.

Eddy Chibás died 11 days later, on August 26, 1951. Castro took his body to display at the university. When it came time to take the corpse to the cemetery, Castro urged José Pardo Llada to help him take the body to the palace instead. Castro wanted to place Chibás on the presidential chair, then Pardo would declare himself president and Castro would declare himself chief of the army. Pardo Llada told him he was crazy.

In 1952 Fidel Castro was prepared to run as an Ortodoxo congressional candidate in Cuban elections. It was the closest he would ever come to participating in democracy.

With their motto Integrity Versus Money, the Ortodoxo Party appeared to be favoured in the 1952 elections. Consequently Batista, still supported by the U.S., arrived at Camp Columbia and took control of the army on March 10. The government of Cuba was toppled in about an hour. Only two people died. Batista's military coup prevented elections in 1952 and suspended the constitution.

In retaliation, the presidential palace was attacked by the *Directorio Revolucionario.* Another student action group, the *Movimiento Nationalista Revolucionario,* planned to attack a military base and arrest Batista, but these young dissidents were betrayed and arrested. The Ortodoxo Party planned its own commando raids in reprisal, but Chibás's successor, Dr. Pelayo Ceurvo, was murdered by Batista's secret police. Other Ortodoxo leaders sought asylum.

Someone had to fight back.

Fidel Castro went into hiding, initially at the home of his half-sister Lidia, but soon filed a brief in the Court of Constitutional Guarantees to have Batista's takeover declared illegal. He called for a prison sentence of 100 years and began organizing his own resistance movement. In the aftermath of the coup, he received some help from a surprising source.

Natalie "Naty" Fernández Revuelta was the beautiful blond

wife of a wealthy cardiologist named Orlando Fernández Ferrer. Born in 1925 and educated in Philadelphia and Washington, D.C., she was a member of the Havana Country Club and the Havana Yacht Club. After the suicide of Eduardo Chibás, without having met Fidel Castro, she provided three sets of keys to her home to be used by Ortodoxo leaders, requesting that one key be given to Fidel Castro.

The dynamic, green-eyed Naty had married a man old enough to be her father after he had treated her for a serious heart ailment. Although she excelled at social gatherings and sports, she was an avid reader of serious literature and a passionate admirer of Chibás. After Chibás shot himself, she couldn't sleep. "The next morning at dawn, I dressed in black and went to the radio station. There was blood everywhere. It was the blood of Chibás's integrity. I touched it. I looked at my bloody hands and knew that unless I found a way to fight injustice, I would feel guilty all my life."

Naty and Fidel met for the first time on November 27 during a public protest to mark the anniversary of the execution of eight medical students in 1871. She attended this demonstration with a clandestine women's organization, Mujueres Martianas, not knowing they would meet. Castro was standing on the grand staircase of the University of Havana. He thanked her for sending him a key to her home.

With some approval from her husband, Naty used family resources to finance Fidel Castro's plans to disrupt and dislodge Batista. Castro told Naty, "I am placing you on an altar inside my heart." While Myrta struggled to raise Fidelito, Fidel Castro was organizing a disciplined inner circle of commandos known as *Fidelistas*. They staged a dramatic torchlight parade to mark the centennial of Martí's birth in January, then an emboldened Castro set his sights on greater glory.

On July 26, 1953, when he was 26, Fidel Castro led an attack on the country's second-largest military installation, the Moncada Army Barracks in Santiago de Cuba.

As dramatic as it was foolhardy, this gesture of defiance clearly established him as the leading dissident in Cuba and gave rise to the July 26 Movement.

Castro's party consisted of approximately 120 men (estimates vary widely) and two women; the Moncada barracks had approximately 1,000 soldiers. Castro planned a simultaneous attack on a much smaller military installation in Bayamo.

In Havana, Naty volunteered to distribute copies of a manifesto that Castro had prepared to be broadcast over the Santiago radio station in eastern Cuba. Fidel's words would be accompanied by the inspiring music of Beethoven, Prokofiev, Mahler, Dvorák and Berlioz, as chosen by Naty, soon after his victory.

With a budget of $20,000, Castro bought shotguns and .22 rifles. He had Cuban army uniforms made for his men to fool the guards. While 27 rebels went to Bayamo, the others went to attack Moncada. The dual attack was planned for 5:15 a.m. after a carnival night, on the assumption that many of the soldiers would be drunk or hungover.

A small contingent of 10 men led by Raúl was to occupy the roof of the Justice Building; a doctor and 20 others, led by Abel Santamaría, would secure the hospital and be prepared to tend the wounded. Fidel would lead the others in a motorcade to the main building where his men would shout at the guards, "Make way for the general!"

Unfamiliar with the streets, many of the rebels became lost on their way to the rendezvous. This back-up group, which had most of the heavier weapons, never arrived. After an advance group had successfully gained entry at Gate Three, a group of 45 men under Castro ran into an outside patrol with machine guns. As Castro's men quickly left their vehicles, shots were fired and the surprise element was gone.

The men in the advance vehicle were already inside the barracks as Fidel Castro and his men were forced to retreat. In the confusion, 33 government soldiers were killed. "I believe we made a mistake by dividing the commando unit we had so carefully trained," Castro wrote. "If our forces had been distributed differently the outcome of the battle might have been different." (Batista's regime soon filled in the bullet holes in the barracks; Castro later had the bullet holes re-created and turned Moncada into a school and a major museum for Cuban history.)

Of the attackers, approximately 50 escaped completely. Only a few of Castro's commandos were killed in direct combat; dozens of others were tortured and shot in captivity. Details of the government's vicious treatment of the prisoners inflamed Cuba. The death toll for the rebels rose as government troops continued to murder their captives.

As one of the survivors who temporarily avoided capture, Castro tried to hide for several days in the Sierra Maestra foothills. On Saturday, August 1, Castro and his two remaining companions, José Suárez and Oscar Alcalde, were surprised in their sleep and arrested by a middle-aged black lieutenant named Pedro Sarría and approximately a dozen men. "The soldiers wanted to kill us," Castro recalls. "They were enraged and were looking for any pretext."

Lieutenant Sarría saved his life, twice. "If we'd given them our names," Castro recalls, "we would have been shot then and there." The lieutenant kept repeating to the other men, "Don't shoot. You can't kill ideas. You can't kill ideas." Impressed, Castro confided his identity to Sarría. The lieutenant advised him to keep his identity secret.

Sarría put the prisoners into the back of a truck, except for Castro, who rode with him in the cab. Sarría's truck was stopped by Major Pérez Chaumont, known for his bloodthirstiness. This major ordered Sarría to take his prisoners to the garrison; instead, Sarría disobeyed and took them to the city jail in Santiago de Cuba.

"If we'd been taken to the garrison," Castro says, "they would have put us through a meat grinder." (Sarría was discharged from Batista's army. Following the revolution he was reinstated and promoted to captain. In 1959 Sarría served as head of security in the presidential palace. He died of cancer in 1972.)

Castro claimed that more than 60 rebels were captured around Santiago de Cuba. Exact numbers are not possible to confirm, but it is incontestible that many prisoners were killed. He collected eyewitness accounts of atrocities from the likes of Andrés García, a survivor of the attack in Bayamo, and built a case against Batista to affirm the right of rebellion against tyranny.

Raúl Castro

As a lawyer, Castro defended Batista's other prisoners. His brother Raúl and Pedro Miret received 13 years, the longest sentences. Twenty men received ten years; three others received three years. The two women involved in the uprising, Melba Hernández, a young lawyer, and Haydée Santamaría, received the lightest sentences, less than a year each, and were sent to a women's prison outside Havana.

In a separate trial in the following October, Castro defended himself. During his five-hour self-defence, he delivered the now-famous speech setting forth his demands for a new and free Cuba.

"The problem of the land, the problem of industrialization, the problem of housing, the problem of unemployment, the problem of education and the problem of people's health; these are the six problems we would take immediate steps to solve, along with the restoration of civil liberties and political democracy," he said.

He proposed to re-institute the 1940 constitution, give ownership of small plots of land to subsistence

Haydée Santamaria

farmers and squatters, give workers a 30-percent share of profits from major industries, provide planters with a 55-percent share of sugar production and confiscate "ill-gotten gains" from previous regimes, corporations and aristocrats.

A fifth "revolutionary law" would subsidize retirement funds and finance public hospitals, asylums and charities. Castro outlined the plight of Cuba's poor, calling for agricultural reforms and universal education. "Cuba, with a population of five and a half million," he said, "has a greater number of unemployed than France or Italy with a population of forty million each."

He claimed Cuba could easily provide for a population three times greater. Markets could be overflowing with produce; all hands could be working. "What is inconceivable is that anyone should go to bed hungry while there is a single inch of unproductive land; that children should die for lack of medical attention. What is inconceivable is that 30 percent of our farm people cannot write their names and that 99 percent of them know nothing of Cuba's history.

"What is inconceivable is that the majority of our rural people are now living in worse circumstances than the Indians Columbus discovered in the fairest land that human eyes had ever seen."

Castro accused Batista of being the worst dictator in Cuban history. "Dante divided his *Inferno* into nine circles," Castro said, vilifying Batista. "He put the criminals in the seventh, the thieves in the eighth and the traitors in the ninth. Difficult dilemma the devils will be faced with, when they try to find an adequate spot for this man's soul—if this man has a soul."

Castro's rhetoric echoed the ideas of José Martí, Tom Paine, Saint Thomas Aquinas, Martin Luther, John Milton, John Locke and Jean-Jacques Rousseau—to name but a few—helping to make him a folk hero throughout the country. His descriptions of butchery and torture were equally effective in fanning revulsion for Batista and his soldiers.

"They crushed their testicles and they tore out their eyes. But no one yielded. Even when they had been deprived of their virile organs, our men were still a thousand times more men than their tormentors together.

"Frustrated by the valor of the men, they tried to break the spirit of our women. With a bleeding human eye in their hands, a sergeant and several other men went to the cell where our comrades Melba Hernández and Haydée Santamaría were held.

"Addressing the latter, and showing her the eye, they said, 'This eye belonged to your brother. If you do not tell us what he refused to say, we will tear out the other.' She, who loved her valiant brother above all things, replied full of dignity: 'If you tore out an eye and he did not speak, much less will I.'"

Near the summation of his oration, Castro asked the judge to reunite him with his comrades. "I cannot ask freedom for myself while my comrades are already suffering in the ignominious prison of the Isle of Pines. Please send me there to join them and to share their fate. It is understandable that honest men should be dead or in prison in a Republic where the President is a criminal and a thief."

Fidel Castro was sentenced to 15 years in prison. In 1953 he was sent to the notorious *Presidio Modelo,* the model prison, on the Island of Pines, as he'd requested. Built under the direction of General Machado in 1931, the prison consisted of five circular buildings directly modelled on an institution in Joliett, Illinois. The inmates' buildings had six floors with 93 cells per floor. Castro's hero José Martí had been incarcerated in 1871 on the same island off the southern coast, *Isla de Pinos.* Its isolated locale served as the geographical basis for Robert Louis Stevenson's *Treasure Island.*

The insurrectionists were kept in a separate section of the prison. Under Castro's direction, his Moncada colleagues adopted a self-disciplinary code of behaviour, impressing the guards. They played songs on a guitar (now enshrined with their signatures in the Museum of the Revolution) while Castro studied the works of Marx and the history of successful peasant uprisings.

"I was isolated from the others until the end of our prison terms," he says. "I'd been kept in solitary confinement in Santiago de Cuba until I was tried, so I must have spent nineteen of the twenty-two months I was in prison in solitary. Near the end, my isolation was ended because they sent Raúl to the place where I was, several months before the amnesty."

In fact, Castro was well treated and respected, often referred to as Dr. Castro in the prison. He had access to his colleagues and participated in the educational classes that the Moncada prisoners organized. Their little school within the prison was dubbed the "Abel Santamaría Ideological Academy" in honour of their fallen comrade.

Castro had visitors, among them his wife Myrta, who smuggled messages to and from the prison. Her brother, Rafael Díaz-Bart, became angry when he learned that Myrta was being coerced into clandestine political activity. Employed by the Batista regime, Rafael managed to provide Myrta with a stipend so she could live and feed her baby; when Castro learned that Myrta was essentially on the government payroll, he was furious. Although he himself had accepted $1,000 from Batista for their honeymoon, Castro preferred his wife and child to live in poverty rather than receive tainted money.

In prison Castro reworked his trial dissertation for an essay entitled "History Will Absolve Me." To do so, he supposedly wrote the text with lime juice on various letters and scraps of paper. When his two female cohorts were released in February of 1954, they ironed the sheets of paper to reveal the lime-juice wording. He wanted 100,000 copies printed. "We thought he had gone out of his mind in prison," Haydée Santamaría said many years later. (One of the revolution's most devoted followers of Castro, Haydée Santamaría committed suicide in 1980, blowing her brains out on July 26, after Castro gave her husband permission to re-marry and allegedly referred to her as "old and doddering.")

Several thousand copies of Castro's text were secretly published, but the speech didn't become famous until after the revolution. Its title was drawn from Castro's summation. "Sentence me. I don't mind. History will absolve me." (The anti-Castro biographer Georgie Anne Geyer has taken pains to point out some similarities between Castro's self-righteous manifesto after his Moncada failure and Adolf Hitler's speech at the close of the Rathaus Putsch trial in 1924 in the aftermath of a similarly quixotic attempt to overrun the War Ministry in Munich. She also notes many dictators such as Castro have emerged "from ignored outskirts of empire." Franco, Galicia. Castro, Oriente. Napoleon, Corsica. Stalin, Georgia. Hitler, Austria.)

During his imprisonment, Castro and Naty Fernández corresponded ardently for almost two years. They ostensibly exchanged opinions on literature, philosophy and religion, but it was also a mutual and skillful courtship. The censor at the prison was sympathetic to Castro, so it remains a mystery as to how one of Castro's letters intended for Naty was sent to his wife. In response to the mix-up, Myrta Díaz-Balart filed for divorce; Naty temporarily backed off to preserve her integrity and social standing. (Naty's husband, Dr. Orlando Fernández, would eventually leave the country with their elder, legitimate daughter after Castro's regime nationalized his health clinic.)

In the wake of his re-election in May of 1955, Batista made an error of enormous historical significance. Responding to public pressure and the demands of the Ortodoxo Party, Batista reluctantly signed an amnesty bill for Cuban political prisoners on May 6.

Upon his release on May 15, Fidel Castro vehemently denounced Batista in the press. He had already launched lawsuits against Batista and three of his commanders. On June 12 he secretly founded an 11-member directorate for *Movimento 26 de Julio* with himself as the leader.

In Havana Castro also pursued his *amistad amorosa,* his loving friendship, with Naty Fernández. They met for illicit rendezvous in an apartment rented by Castro's half-sister, Lidia.

After a warrant was issued for Raúl Castro in connection with a bomb blast, Castro accused Batista's regime of planning to murder him and his brother. Raúl Castro took refuge in the Mexican embassy in Havana for a week before flying to Mexico City on June 24. Fidel Castro was banned from making radio broadcasts, and then the authorities shut down a daily newspaper, *La Calle,* that had served Castro as a propaganda outlet.

Fidel Castro followed his brother into self-imposed exile in Mexico on July 7, 1955, arriving in Vera Cruz and traveling to the United States in an effort to raise funds that could support a revolution. Lidia Castro sold her refrigerator to assist him with travel money.

In 1956, while Fidel Castro was in Mexico, he became a father for a second time. Castro's daughter, Alina Fernández, was born in Havana on March 19 to Naty Fernández Revuelta. The child was christened Alina, meaning "to Lina," to curry favour with Castro and Castro's mother, Lina. Castro had Lidia examine the baby to confirm that family birthmarks were present.

Before leaving Cuba, Fidel Castro had asked Naty to accompany him. Pregnant and pressured by her mother, she had turned him down. Castro never forgave her. He referred to the Díaz-Balarts as "Judases" and disdainfully said that Naty Fernández Revuelta had "missed the boat." Twelve years later, when Castro was finally prepared to offer his surname to Alina, the girl decided to keep the name Fernández.

Alina Fernández never knew her father's direct phone number. Although Castro sometimes visited her mother's home when she was little, she visited his house only once. He occasionally sent gifts, such as a complete set of Balzac in French, a doll that looked like him and a live Russian bear. She was once summoned after midnight to watch him play basketball; another time he took her to a theatre to watch newsreel footage about himself. Mostly he ignored her. "Alina was a minor player in his pageant of egotism," notes family biographer Wendy Gimbel.

For Alina's wedding in 1972, Castro provided four bottles of rum for the guests, a bottle of scotch for himself and a pasta salad decorated with a pineapple.

Over the years, as an outspoken dissident in Cuba, Alina was admonished by her father but never jailed. Anorexic and divorced after four short marriages ("I'm an annual, not a perennial"), she began her efforts to leave Cuba in 1988.

After she married a Mexican businessman, her father refused her permission to emigrate. With a false passport, disguised as a Spanish tourist, Alina Fernández finally left Cuba for the United States in 1993, leaving behind her only daughter, Mumin, who later moved to Miami with her father. (Juanita Castro, Fidel Castro's sister, had defected on June 29, 1964. The *New York Times* later reported she had been on the CIA's payroll since 1960.)

Alina Fernández led a demonstration by Cuban-American exiles when Castro arrived in New York for the fiftieth anniversary of the United Nations in 1995. She settled in Madrid, where she wrote *Castro's Daughter: An Exile's Memoir of Cuba*.

Alina Fernández has described her father as an "assassin," a "mediocrity" and "Mr. Power." She says, "My father's island is nothing but an enormous prison."

CHE AND MEXICO

In Mexico City in 1955, the Castro brothers met a young Argentinian doctor named Ernesto Guevara.

Born in Rosario, Argentina, on June 14, 1928, Ernesto Guevara de la Serna was the son of a seldom-employed construction engineer and failed plantation owner, Ernesto Guevara

Lynch, of Irish descent, and his wife, Celia de la Serna, of Spanish descent. At age two he contracted severe asthma, which plagued him for the rest of his life.

The Guevara family moved to Buenos Aires, but the climate proved inhospitable to young Ernesto, so they resettled in Cordoba province, at Alta Gracia, where he learned French from his mother. In 1946 he moved with his family back to Buenos Aires, where he enrolled in the faculty of medicine, specializing in allergies. Believing that "willpower can overcome anything," he was determined to find a cure for his crippling and painful asthma.

During his youth, Ernesto was a shameless seducer of girls and women, a *caradura,* and a notoriously sloppy dresser who earned the nickname "the pig." With a cavalier attitude to cleanliness as well as women, he also enjoyed shocking his father and the Argentinian gentry with his combative intellect. But beyond his rambunctious proselytizing in favour of social change, he stayed on the political sidelines and continued to fraternize with the gentry.

To understand society better he went on a marathon bicycle tour of Argentina in 1950, traveling 2,500 miles in six weeks, alone, on a bicycle outfitted with a little Italian Cucchiolo engine. Later that year—it was his fourth year of medical school—he fell in love with 16-year-old Maria del Carmen "Chichina" Ferreyra, the beautiful daughter of one of the wealthiest and oldest families in Cordoba. He wanted to marry her, but Chichina's family would not approve the union.

In 1952 he began a vagabond journey around South America, initially by motorcycle, accompanied by his friend Alberto Grenado. This trip was extremely influential in formulating his anti-American, anti-imperialist views. In particular, his visit to the Chuquicamata copper mine in Chile heightened his disdain for Americans as "blonde, efficient and insolent masters."

Deported from Colombia, Guevara and Grenado continued to Venezuela, from where Ernesto traveled alone to Miami. Summoned home for compulsory military service, he was rejected due to his asthmatic condition. He completed his medical studies in 1953, specializing in leprosy and allergic diseases.

Ernesto Guevara worked in a leprosy hospital in Venezuela, then went to Guatemala in 1954 with a friend, Ricardo Roji, to help the progressive government of Jacobo Arbenz. At age 25 he openly joined in a political struggle for the first time.

While watching the CIA-sponsored militia topple Guatemala's democratically elected leader, Guevara wrote several articles, including "I Saw Jacobo Arbenz Fall," and crystallized his views of American imperialism during his six months in Guatemala.

In Guatemala City he also planned a manual for doctors in a revolution to be titled "The Role of the Doctor in Latin America," and met his future first wife, the older Hilda Gadea, a Peruvian political exile who showed a maternal interest in his asthma. She was not a great beauty, but she had leftist sympathies and a willingness to make sacrifices for him.

In Guatemala he also met Antonio "Nico" López, a participant in the ill-fated attack on the Moncada and Bayama army barracks. López had evaded capture and found refuge in the Guatemalan embassy in Havana. Granted asylum by Arbenz in Guatemala, López enthusiastically described the young lawyer Fidel Castro Ruz to Guevara.

It was Nico López who began to refer to Ernesto Guevara as "Che." He did so in response to the doctor's own habit of using the word *Che,* a common Argentinian term that essentially means "Hey you."

Ernesto "Che" Guevara took refuge in the Argentinian embassy upon the arrival of the designated "liberator" of Guatemala, Castilla Armas, who was accompanied by U.S. Ambassador John Puerifoy, in April. Jacobo Arbenz was first stripped of his power, then literally stripped at the airport prior to leaving for exile in Mexico.

Che resolved to follow Arbenz and other Guatemalan dissidents to Mexico City. Escaping across the border to Mexico in September had the added benefit of liberating the cavalier Che from the matrimonial advances of Hilda Gadea. While volunteering at the General Hospital, Che accidently met Nico López once more. In Mexico City, López had assembled a coterie of would-be revolutionaries at the home of a professional Mexican wrestler named "Dick" Medrano.

Che was soon invited to join López's social circle and was reunited with Hilda, who was in an advanced stage of pregnancy. (They were married in August of 1955 and honeymooned in Chiapas and the Yucatan. She gave birth to a daughter, Hilda Beatriz, on February 15, 1956. Guevara's pet names for the child were "Hildita" and "My little Mao.")

Nico López returned briefly to Havana to re-connect with the Castro brothers after their release from the Island of Pines prison. Consequently, when Raúl Castro came to Mexico City on June 24, he reunited with López.

Raúl Castro first met Che Guevara at 49 Calle Emparan, the home of Medrano and his Cuban wife, Maria Antonia. Although Guevara was never an ardent physician, he treated Raúl Castro for the flu. Politically compatible, the two men became friends.

In the summer of 1955 a young Soviet Foreign Ministry representative named Nikolai Leonov bumped into Raúl Castro in Mexico City when they were shopping. Leonov and Raúl

Castro had met first in 1953 on a ship while Raúl was returning from Europe. Without obtaining permission from his embassy, Leonov visited an address Raúl had given him, thereby initiating a link that would develop into a Soviet-Cuban alliance. The Russian attaché Leonov befriended several Cuban exiles and Che Guevara.

Fidel Castro arrived in Mexico on July 7. Upon their first meeting, Che Guevara and Fidel Castro talked intensively about Cuba and revolution. Castro invited Che to join his group and he immediately accepted.

Castro went to visit the Cuban émigré communities in Florida, New York, Philadelphia and New Jersey to raise funds for their planned military assault on Cuba. "I can inform you with complete reliability," Castro told 800 people in New York, "that in 1956 we will be free or we will be martyrs."

On June 20, 1956, Fidel Castro was arrested on the street in downtown Mexico City by Mexican police. He was accused of plotting to assassinate Batista with the help of Cuban and Mexican communists. Castro denied having strong Communist Party affiliations. Fifty other arrests were made. Raúl Castro went into hiding; Che Guevara remained at the movement's training ranch 35 miles east of the city.

On June 24 Che Guevara was arrested, ostensibly for over-staying his visa. The Argentinian doctor was widely viewed in the media as one of the most dangerous of the would-be revolution-aries. Whereas Castro was wary of making any reckless remarks that might incite the Eisenhower White House to suspect an upsurge of communism, Che frankly discussed his Marxist beliefs with the police.

Che refused to use his privileged diplomatic connections to secure his own release. He and Fidel were photographed in their

shared prison cell. After considerable efforts were made to exon-
erate Castro, a judge ordered his release on July 2. Castro was
eventually freed on July 26, thanks to sympathetic intervention
by Mexico's former president Lazaro Cardenas.

Che Guevara, "honest to a fault," remained incarcerated. He
urged Fidel to leave Mexico and carry out their plans without
him. Fidel, in turn, pledged that he would not abandon his
friend. Che penned a poem, "Canto a Fidel," expressing his deep
loyalty and appreciation. Impressed by Che's intrepid nature,
Castro used the movement's precious funds to bribe Mexican
police and gain the release of the final two detainees, Che and
Calixto García, after their two months of captivity.

For three months, while Fidel finalized plans for his invasion,
the rebels went underground instead of leaving Mexico, as
ordered by the courts. Short of money, Castro was forced to
travel illegally into Texas to meet an ex-president of Cuba, Carlos
Prío Socarrás, whom he had often accused of corruption. It has
been reported that Castro easily swam across the Rio Grande to
attend the meeting in the border town of McAllen.

Although Prío was not aligned with Castro in terms of ideol-
ogy, Prío hoped to generate sufficient unrest in Cuba to allow
him to enjoy a resurgence of influence or perhaps even control.
Prío contributed more than $50,000 to the cause. (Some
evidence suggests Prío was acting in concert with the CIA; Castro
biographer Tad Szulc, however, believes the CIA didn't provide
any direct funding for Castro until 1957 or 1958.) The Prío
donation was enough for Castro to purchase a second-hand, 38-
foot motor yacht, *Granma,* constructed in 1943 in Mexico and
named in honour of the first owner's grandmother.

The awkwardly spelled *Granma* was sold by American expa-
triate Robert Erickson on the condition that Castro would also

purchase Erickson's riverside house in the Mexican port town of Tuxpan. The combined purchase price was $40,000. Castro made a down payment.

Castro received coastal charts for his planned invasion of Cuba from Celia Sánchez, the 37-year-old daughter of a Cuban plantation doctor who greatly admired José Martí. This was the beginning of her many years of providing unprecedented guidance and ardent counsel to Castro, whose passions and egotism often lacked prudence.

In 1953, to mark the one hundredth anniversary of Martí's birth, Celia and her father had climbed Cuba's

Celia Sánchez

highest peak, Pico Turquino, and erected a bust of Martí, the "Apostle of Pico Turquino." With Celia acting as his press agent, Castro would climb the same 6,507-foot peak in 1957 to give a filmed CBS interview that Celia coordinated. Only months after the revolution succeeded, government trainees had to climb Turquino Peak at regular intervals. According to Reinaldo Arenas, to become an agricultural accountant, a trainee had to climb the mountain six times; to join the diplomatic service required 25 climbs.

Active in the successful campaign to free the Moncada prisoners, Sánchez was diligently preparing an underground network in the sierra from her home base in Pilon, southwest of Manzanillo, in association with Frank País, a 21-year-old student who became Fidel Castro's official coordinator in Oriente. País visited Fidel Castro twice in Mexico City in 1956, in August and October. His father was the pastor of the First Baptist Church in Santiago de Cuba. Modest, handsome, sensible, honest and serious, País had already distinguished himself with his group called *Acción Nacional Revolucionaria.* At Castro's insistence, he agreed to lead and organize an uprising in Santiago de Cuba to coincide with the arrival of the *Granma.*

Castro's men in Mexico received their combat training from Alberto Bayo. Born in Camaguey, Cuba, in 1892, Bayo had fought in the Spanish Civil War against Franco. He lost his right eye in Africa, where he had been a captain in the Spanish Foreign Legion. Convinced by Castro's revolutionary zeal, Bayo sold his furniture factory in Mexico to support the movement. Bayo accepted the task of secretly training Castro's *guerrilleros,* imposing strict discipline.

The Spanish Civil War was also the connection between Castro and one of his chief allies in Mexico, the beautiful and artistic Teresa "Teté" Casuso. As the Cuban widow of the famous poet Pablo de la Torriente, who had been killed fighting for the Republicans in Spain, she first visited the would-be liberators when they were marooned in prison.

With Teté on that visit was an elegant, 16-year-old Spanish beauty, Isabel Custodio. Upon his release from prison, Fidel Castro obsessively stalked and wooed her. The one-sided courtship continued for two months. He gradually wore down her resistance and proposed marriage. She accepted and moved back to live with her parents; Castro also followed the bourgeois conventions.

While Fidel Castro was buying and stockpiling munitions at Teté's house, he was also buying a trousseau and a bottle of French perfume for his hesitant fiancée, Isabel. He also bought her a conservative bathing suit because he disapproved of her immodest French bikini. To emphasize his ardour, Fidel Castro invited Isabel Custodio to be the only woman to join his invasionary force on the *Granma*. She declined and broke the engagement.

On November 26, 1956, 82 men wearing their M-26 armbands left the Mexican port of Tuxpan on the overloaded *Granma*. They hoped to land at a deserted beach named Playa las Coloradas near Niquero in Oriente on November 30. On a vessel designed to carry only 25 people, many of the 82 men were seasick. Food and water rations were used up. The boat leaked. One engine failed. Their navigator fell overboard. Encountering choppy seas, the inexperienced mariners took seven days to complete the crossing, instead of the five Fidel Castro had planned.

The failure to arrive on time had deadly consequences for Frank País's men, who had begun their insurrection on November 30 as prearranged, to coincide with Castro's landing. After taking control of the streets in Santiago de Cuba and issuing a proclamation, many of Frank País's comrades were killed. The courageous uprising only served to alert Batista to Castro's anticipated invasion.

In 1979 the official Cuban version of Castro's *Granma* expedition, *De Tuxpan a La Plata,* would describe the popular uprising as a political victory. But the invasion of Cuba by Fidel Castro was, at first, as inept as his invasion of the Moncada Army Barracks.

3 | CASTRO'S GLORY

Earliest picture of Fidel Castro invading Cuba in 1956: "Above all, we are fighting for a democratic Cuba and an end to the dictatorship"

THE *GRANMA* LANDED AT a swamp about 100 miles west of Santiago, at the Gulf of Guacanayabo, at 5 a.m. on December 2, 1956. When the yacht struck a sandbar near Purgatory Point, more than a mile from their intended destination, the rebels had to wade ashore and leave most of their weapons and supplies behind.

It was a disastrous beginning. Che Guevara referred to their landing as a shipwreck. Saltwater had oxidized some of the gun parts. Airplanes were soon attacking. Celia Sánchez had nervously waited for two nights with Crescencio Pérez, the area's leading marijuana grower, to provide transportation for Castro's men to the Sierra Maestra. On the morning of December 2, Pérez's trucks found a few invaders hiding in an ice plant at Niquero.

Disoriented, most of the seasick revolutionaries were slaughtered by Batista's troops three days later, on December 5, at the edge of a sugarcane field at Alegría de Pío. The rebels tried to flee in panic. Many abandoned their weapons. Che Guevara was wounded in the neck by a deflected bullet. "I lost hope for a couple of minutes," he wrote in his diary.

The 15 men who were able to escape into the mountains were Fidel Castro Ruz, Faustino Pérez Hernández, Universe Sánchez Alvarez, Raúl Castro Ruz, Ciro Redondo Garcia, Rene Rodríguez Cruz, Efigenio Amejeiras Delgado, Armando Rodríguez Moya, Ivan Almeida Bosque, Ernesto Guevara de la Serna, Ramiro Valdés Menéndez, Rafael Choa Sanliana, Camilo Cienfuengos Corriaran, Reinaldo Benitez Napoles and Francisco Gonzalez Hemandez.

Separated and without food or water, some men drank their urine and ate raw corn and crabs. They traveled in small groups by moonlight and hid during the day. A peasant named Guillermo García rounded up the hideaways. On December 21,

15 men reassembled in the Sierra Maestra with only nine weapons between them. (There would be 18 men in total, according to Fidel Castro, who would ultimately evade capture—not *La Doce* or "the Twelve," as later noted with biblical gravity by some pro-Castro accounts.)

Granma

Among the dead were Nico López and Juan Manuel Márquez, Castro's friend who had accompanied him on his fund-raising tour of the U.S. Having reached the Sierra Maestra, Fidel Castro was nonetheless enthused and confident of victory.

Castro severely castigated the men who had lost their rifles, including Che Guevara. Stung by this reproach, Che suffered an asthma attack. The following day Castro confiscated Che's pistol and gave it to the *guajiro* strongman Crescencio Pérez. That same day the rebels were equipped with four submachine guns and carbines sent from Manzanillo by Celia Sánchez.

Given an inferior carbine, Che was anxious to redeem himself. He had to wait until the wee hours of January 16 for the rebels' first raid on a military outpost. Two soldiers were killed, five were wounded, and weapons and food were seized. The battle for Cuban sovereignty was underway. As a severely asthmatic non-Cuban with an aristocratic background, Che Guevara shot and killed his first soldier at close range on January 22.

One of the *Granma* survivors, Faustino Pérez, left the Sierra Maestra on Castro's instructions, disguised as a local *guajiro* in a straw hat. He made it all the way to Havana where he raised $30,000. As word spread throughout Cuba that Fidel Castro was alive and free, sympathizers traveled to Oriente province to join with the rebels. The rebels' first fatality in combat was an illiterate black peasant, Julio Zenon Acosta, who had been learning the alphabet from Che Guevara. Later Guevara commemorated Acosta as "my first pupil."

A meeting of Castro's National Directorate on February 16 was unforgettable for both Castro brothers for both romantic and political reasons.

One of the women who arrived for the summit was Vilma Espín, 27. An MIT-educated daughter of a rich Santiago de Cuba family, she had participated in the uprising led by Frank País. She would become Raúl Castro's wife (later separated), the mother of his four children and the head of the Federation of Cuban Women.

Another woman who arrived that day was Celia Sánchez, meeting Fidel Castro for the first time. Some members of her family were horrified that she had left home at age 29 to live with the rebels. She would become Secretary of the Central Committee of the Communist Party of Cuba and Secretary of the Council of State. Equally significant, she was also to become Fidel Castro's indispensable secretary, his alleged lover and his most trusted and non-sycophantic confidante.

Vilma Espín

A CBS journalist who met them in the Sierra Maestra later observed, "She's the only person to whom Castro shows an unashamed need." Having met them after the Revolution had succeeded, French journalist Michel Tourguy commented, "Her saint was Fidel, and she was his muse. It was one of those historic relationships."

Celia Sánchez had worked with Faustino Pérez in Havana to orchestrate the arrival in the camp on February 17 of *New York Times* correspondent Herbert Matthews. More influential than any battle, Matthews's positive coverage of Castro's campaign, in a series of three articles, was orchestrated with daring, foresight and trickery.

As Castro's designated emissary, Faustino Pérez had visited the home of Felipe Pazos, the country's leading economist, in early February. To prove to an incredulous Pazos that Fidel Castro was really alive, Pérez ingeniously suggested that a foreign journalist could be sent to the Sierra Maestra to confirm it.

The economist Pazos contacted the *New York Times* bureau chief in Havana, Ruby Hart Phillips. She in turn suggested the services of Herbert Matthews, a senior *New York Times* correspondent, who happened to be coming to Havana on February 9 for a vacation with his wife. Matthews had covered Chiang Kai-shek in Peking, Mussolini's campaign in Abyssinia (Ethiopia) in 1935, the Spanish Civil War and World War II. When contacted by the Havana bureau chief, Matthews agreed to put his holiday plans on hold.

By arranging for coverage from the *New York Times,* Celia Sánchez was replicating the approach of her hero, José Martí, who had been interviewed by a war correspondent for the *New York Herald,* George E. Bryson, prior to Martí's arrival in Cuba in 1895. This publicity coup was integral to the political coup that followed.

With fewer than 20 armed men, Castro needed the *New York Times* to overestimate the strength of his forces. During a three-hour interview with Matthews on February 17, Castro arranged to have a rebel fighter burst into their camp with a message from "the Second Column." He also arranged to have the same men repeatedly march past as they talked. Matthews was thoroughly taken with Castro, who said everything he thought the outside world wanted to hear.

"You can be sure we have no animosity towards the United States," Castro told Matthews. "Above all, we are fighting for a democratic Cuba and an end to the dictatorship."

Matthews romantically echoed Hemingway when he wrote, "A bell tolled in the jungle of the Sierra Maestra." His sympathetic view of the rebels swayed world opinion against Batista. After the first article appeared on February 24, Batista publicly claimed that the interview with Castro was a fabrication and that Castro was really dead. The *New York Times* subsequently published a photograph of Matthews and Castro together, smoking cigars.

In response to this public relations triumph, the U.S. ambassador to Cuba, Arthur Gardner, suggested to President Dwight D. Eisenhower that the CIA assassinate Fidel Castro. But Eisenhower and Ambassador Gardner were slow off the mark. A would-be assassin was already in Castro's camp even before Matthews's interview.

Eutimio Guerra was a peasant guide who had slept side by side with Castro under the same blanket in January. According to legend, he had a Colt pistol and two hand grenades, but he lacked the courage to kill Castro and collect a $10,000 payment from the army. Guerra's traitorous behaviour was detected after he was granted permission to temporarily return to visit his family.

Che Guevara had repeatedly volunteered for dangerous assignments and had become a formidable interrogator on behalf of the group. He was also acutely suspicious of new recruits and rigorously intolerant of cowardice. When it was confirmed beyond any doubt that Eutimio Guerra was an informer, nobody else wished to undertake the cold-blooded execution of the revolution's first traitor on February 17.

The job fell to Che Guevara.

During a tropical rainstorm, shortly after Guerra had returned to camp, Che stepped forward and shot Guerra with a .32-calibre pistol in the right side of the brain "to end an uncomfortable situation." Che described the killing in scientific medical terms in his diary. From that day forward, Guevara's reputation as an uncompromising and fearless revolutionary grew. He also became increasingly demanding of others, often judgmental in the extreme.

By July Castro casually informed Che that he, Che, had been promoted to the rank of *Comandante,* the official leader of the rebel army's Second Column, thereby bypassing his brother Raúl for the honour.

More foreign reporters followed Herbert Matthews. One reporter for *Coronet* magazine made five visits. There was even a correspondent from *Boy's Life.* Celia Sánchez managed the finances, correspondence and media traffic for the movement as a one-woman bureaucracy. By protecting and chastising Fidel Castro when necessary, she became his alternate compass. Although sometimes disparaged for her plain looks, she was admired for her kindness and practicality. "Celia stopped a lot of madness," as one of Fidel's bodyguards put it.

The charismatic Castro was winning the public relations war. An unauthorized radio station, *Radio Rebelde,* began transmitting anti-Batista broadcasts. Castro offered soothing pronouncements, defending the rights of free enterprise to mollify the

Americans. "Never has the July 26 Movement talked of socialism or of nationalizing industries," Castro said.

Urban terrorists independent of Castro were disrupting Cuba's elite with bombings and kidnappings. On March 13, 1957, some 35 Cuban students attacked the presidential palace, hoping to assassinate General Batista. Of the student rebels, 32 were killed, including José Antonio Echeverria, a potential rival for Fidel Castro. Batista's apparent enjoyment of his lethal victory over the attackers shifted public opinion; many adherents of santería shifted their allegiances to Fidel. Although the national economic output was rising, sugar prices were dropping, the army was dissatisfied and tourism revenues plummeted with the onset of violence.

Contravening the terms of the Guantánamo lease, the U.S. naval base provided munitions to Batista's forces and allowed government bombers to refuel on the site. Castro's men apprehended a busload of Guantánamo personnel in protest. On May 28, 1957, the rebels took much-needed supplies from Batista's soldiers in a small army outpost at El Uvero.

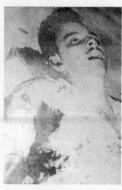

Frank País

The civil unrest in Cuba was exacerbated by the murder of Josué País by the Santiago de Cuba police in June and the murder of his brother, the "National Chief of Action of the 26th of July Movement," Frank País, in broad daylight by Santiago police on July 30, 1957. The latter murder led to strikes in three eastern provinces.

A general strike in April of 1958 further damaged Batista's increasingly tenuous hold on power. Washington withdrew support, instituted an arms embargo and sent a New York banker as an emissary to persuade Batista to step down, but Batista would not cooperate. The American interests were economic, more than social. By 1958 Americans bought more sugar from Cuba than any other country; they provided 75 percent of Cuba's imports; they controlled 80 percent of the public railroads and 90 percent of the telephone and electricity services.

That summer, when Batista launched one final offensive against the rebels, sending 10,000 government troops into the Sierra Maestra, many of his soldiers defected; others deserted, leaving their weapons. After two years in the mountains, having made their permanent headquarters at La Plata where they began broadcasting their messages on Radio Rebelde, Castro's "dozen" comrades had swelled to 50,000 troops, mobilized in two columns, with Camilo Cienfuegos rivalling Fidel Castro as the most effective and determined military leader.

The State Department and the CIA were looking for a replacement for Batista, but it was too late. An estimated 90 percent of Cubans were in favour of the "26th of July Movement." On the evening of December 31, 1958, Batista received an urgent message from his general in Santiago de Cuba warning that Castro was set to take control of the city. Batista responded by gathering his personal fortune, estimated at between $30 million and $40 million, and fleeing the country.

Unknown to casino boss Meyer Lansky, Batista had already requested visas to leave for America at the end of 1958. When the news that Batista was headed for the airport began to circulate on New Year's Eve, the sold-out floorshow at the Copa suddenly had 200 cancellations. That night Batista fled with his fortune to the Dominican Republic, then to Florida, then on to Spain, where he died in 1973.

For Cuba's six million other citizens, a new regime was marching into power.

VICTORY AND RADICAL CHANGE

On January 1, 1959, Fidel Castro took Santiago de Cuba, seizing the Moncada Army Barracks without firing a shot. Che Guevara led a famous victory in Santa Clara, derailing heavily armoured train cars with Molotov cocktails. (Replicas of these rail cars remain on display as a museum in Santa Clara, the city in which Pope John Paul II conducted his first Cuban mass.)

Camilo Cienfuegos
"Lord of the Vanguard"

Camilo Cienfuegos and Che Guevara were the first rebel leaders to arrive in Havana, receiving heroes' welcomes on January 1 and 2. They had hastened to the capital partly to discourage any other rebel factions from claiming control of the city. Of particular concern was the Cuban Communist Party (PSP), which had refused to participate in the general strike in April.

The first, most high-profile entrance was allocated to Cienfuegos for the occupation of the Camp Columbia military headquarters. Contrary to the Castro brothers and Guevara, who were clearly intellectuals, the good-humoured Camilo Cienfuegos was not feared by the Americans or the Cubans to be a communist. As a handsome, fearless man of action, without pretensions to sophistication, the Stetson-wearing, baseball-playing Camilo was a man of the people, once described by Che as "happy, down-to-earth and a joker."

"Camilo also had charisma," Castro says. "If you look at Camilo's picture, you'll see that his bearded face is similar to those of the Apostles."

Having given centre stage to Cienfuegos, Fidel Castro did not arrive in Havana until January 8. During his first victory speech to a huge crowd, a flock of white doves was released. When one of the doves alighted on his shoulder, it was widely accepted by the santería adherents that this was a sign that Fidel Castro had been chosen to deliver Cuba from oppression. Cynics and detractors have suggested that birdseed was placed on Castro's shoulders to encourage the spectacle.

Castro remained coy about his plans. The U.S. government was initially optimistic. Although the triumphant rioters vandalized most of the Mafia's casinos, Castro's government didn't officially outlaw gambling operations until June. Santos Trafficante Jr. and Lansky were deported in July. Trafficante Jr. later sought revenge, but Lansky was philosophical about his losses. "I crapped out," he said.

To distract the Eisenhower administration, Fidel's regime of *barbudos,* or "bearded ones," had Manuel Urrutia, an exiled judge, flown in from Venezuela to serve as Cuba's provisional president. Urrutia had defended Castro and his insurgents during the Moncada Barracks trials. To further confound and mollify world opinion, Urrutia then appointed José Miró Cardona, president of the Havana Bar Association, as the new prime minister. Cardona had links with North American companies and had once defended the corrupt Cuban president Grau San Martín.

Meanwhile, as later reported by dissident writer Reinaldo Arenas in his memoir *Before Night Falls,* young "cadres of the Revolution" were already being indoctrinated with communistic principles as early as the first half of 1960. Arenas recalls that the texts for his Marxism-Leninism courses in 1960 included the *Manual of the USSR Academy of Sciences,* the *Manual of Political Economy* by Nikitin and *Foundations of Socialism in Cuba* by Blas Roca.

In keeping with his plan to allay American concerns, Castro didn't immediately allocate high-profile positions to Che or his brother Raúl, the movement's leftist radicals. Raúl was left in Santiago as the military governor of Oriente province. Che became commander of La Cabana, the fortress at the mouth of Havana's harbour. Cuba officially declared him to be a citizen, thereby enabling him to hold political office.

At age 30 Che was compared to the famous South American liberator José de San Martín in a widely distributed poem by Nicolás Guillén, living in exile in Buenos Aires. (Guillén would return to become the head of the Writers Union and a Castro loyalist, who suppressed literary freedom on behalf of his boss in order to retain his privileged position until 1989.) Meanwhile, Che was solidifying his mystique as a ruthless executioner at home.

Given the job of prosecuting war criminals and deciding the fate of collaborators, Guevara oversaw La Cabana's *Comision de Depuración,* or Cleansing Commission. With Che serving as both chief prosecutor and supreme judge, firing squads executed 55 men in 100 days. Meanwhile, on the other end of the island, Raúl Castro oversaw the mass execution of 70 soldiers. They were lined up in front of a trench, mowed down by machine guns, then bulldozed into the trench.

As a member of the July 26 Movement from Holguin, 15-year-old writer Reinaldo Arenas saw Fidel Castro win a war that he claims had barely been fought. "During my whole time with the rebels, I never took part in any battle; I never even witnessed a battle; those battles were more myth than reality." As soon as the Revolution was declared won, blood began to spill more copiously. "The innocent died with the guilty," Arenas claims. "Many more were dying now than during the war that never was."

Che was adamant that Cuba must not make the same mistake that Arbenz had made in Guatemala. They must not allow disloyal elements to remain in the armed forces, susceptible to CIA infiltration. While some of Che's friends and his visiting father were troubled by his apparent transformation into a merciless man, he had his sights set on a continental revolution, unseating tyrants throughout Latin America. He regarded clemency as dangerous weakness. Instead of celebrating victory, he was already meeting with revolutionary leaders from other countries.

Many Batista loyalists were jailed or executed, and Castro's regime began its intense persecution of homosexuals. Although some high-ranking homosexual members of Castro's regime were immune to imprisonment, homosexuals were increasingly seen as dangerous, anti-social elements. Homosexuals were antithetical to the "New Man" to be modelled in the vainglorious image of macho Che Guevara.

Urrutia's cabinet reformed the constitution and proposed a bill to ban gambling and prostitution. Fidel Castro was opposed to this moralistic legislation because he didn't want to risk alienating the unemployed who favoured the island's "entertainment" industry. When Castro insisted the government re-open the brothels and allow the national lottery to continue, Prime Minister Miró resigned, and Castro, now 32, took his place on February 13.

The government took control of the Cuban Telephone Company, an affiliate of American-owned ITT, and reduced electrical rates paid to the foreign-owned Cuban Electric Company by 30 percent. The Cuban Film Institute was created, prices for medicine were reduced and rents were lowered by 30 to 50 percent in keeping with a new Urban Reform Law.

A new Agrarian Reform Law was introduced to limit land ownership to 1,000 acres. Holdings in excess of that amount would be expropriated and compensations would be paid in 20-year, fixed-term bonds at 4.5 percent, with compensations to be based on assessed values for taxes.

Previously private beaches were opened to the public. (Public use of Cuba's beaches was later restricted, with access apportioned to members of loyalist organizations, newly married couples and party officials, etc. In many areas around Havana and Varadero, swimming reverted to being a privilege, not a right.)

Under Batista, 8 percent of landowners had controlled 70 percent of the land. Foreigners owned 75 percent of arable land. Five sugar companies owned or controlled more than two million acres. When Fidel Castro pressed for the agricultural land reforms, as promised, to limit private ownership, the provisional President Urrutia refused to sign the revolutionary laws, responding to the protests of the National Association of Cattlemen and the Tobacco Growers Association. Urrutia was removed from his post on July 16, 1959. Castro's substitute for president was a July 26 Movement leader from Cienfuegos, Osvaldo Dorticós.

As in Guatemala, big American-owned companies balked at the compensations offered because their own artificially low assessed values, which had enabled them to pay low taxes for decades, did not realistically reflect market values. Although

Cuba eventually negotiated compensation packages with private owners and the governments of Britain, Canada, France, Italy, Spain, Mexico and Sweden, no agreement was reached with the United States.

As in Guatemala, the chief corporate adversary was the United Fruit Company (United Brands, Chiquita Brands). While expropriating 70,000 acres from U.S. sugar companies, Cuba also confiscated 35,000 acres of United Fruit Company property in Oriente province.

By antagonizing the United Fruit Company, Castro was inviting the wrath of CIA-related shareholders and directors. These included John Foster Dulles (Secretary of State and United Fruit counsel), Allen W. Dulles (CIA director and former United Fruit president), Henry Cabot Lodge (UN ambassador and former United Fruit director) and Walter Bedell Smith (former CIA director who had become president of United Fruit after the overthrow of Arbenz in Guatemala.)

In May of 1959 American Vice-President Richard Nixon allegedly met with the Mafia and representatives of the major corporate players in Cuba, which included the United Fruit Company, Pepsi Cola, Ford Motor Company and Standard Oil. In return for their promise of funding support for his candidacy for president, Nixon pledged the United States would oust Castro's regime. (In his article for the *Realist* called "The Kennedy Assassination—The Nixon-Bush Connection?" California private investigator Paul Kangas has attributed direct responsibility for the CIA's plans to invade Cuba to Nixon and connects CIA/Mafia liaisons to Nixon and Texas millionaire George Bush.)

To prevent confiscation of Cuban gold reserves in Fort Knox, Che Guevara, as the newly appointed director of the National Bank of Cuba, transferred the money to Swiss and Canadian banks in November. The story goes that during a cabinet meeting, Fidel Castro supposedly asked for a good *economista*. Che misheard and volunteered for Cuba's top banking job, thinking Fidel had asked for a good *communista*.

While Che Guevara studied economics with Mexican economist Juan Noyola and advanced mathematics with Dr. Vilaseca, he was simultaneously head of the *Instituto Nacional de Reforma Agraria* (INRA), an organization he designed to conceive and implement Cuba's sweeping land reforms.

Castro showed his hand decisively in the "Year of Agrarian Reform" by nationalizing 2.5 million acres. In 1960 he nationalized large, foreign-owned businesses, including oil refineries that had refused to process Soviet crude (Shell, Esso, Texaco). The oil refineries wouldn't cooperate with Castro because they had been threatened into non-compliance by the U.S. Treasury Department.

Castro also nationalized sugar mills and U.S. banks (Chase Manhattan, First National Bank of Boston, First National City Bank of New York). Americans had owned 165 major companies and half of the sugar industry. In retaliation, President Eisenhower cancelled Cuba's sugar quota in July. The Soviet Union came forward to purchase the sugar that the United States would not buy. China, as well, signed a five-year treaty to purchase 500,000 tons of sugar annually.

And in 1960, Cuba nationalized rental housing and some 382 Cuban-owned firms, and withdrew from the World Bank (the International Bank for Reconstruction and Development).

The honeymoon was definitely over.

UNCLE SAM'S SHADOW

The United States advised its citizens living in Cuba to send their families home and advised Americans not to travel to

Cuba. In response Fidel told Americans they were welcome to stay in Cuba.

The tit-for-tat chess game was officially on.

After Cuba's foreign minister approached the UN Security Council and charged the U.S. with planning an invasion, Castro requested that the U.S. embassy reduce its staff to 11, to equal the number at the Cuban embassy in Washington.

Attending the opening of the United Nations in September 1960, Castro was restricted by the Americans to the island of Manhattan, along with Nikita Khrushchev, Hungary's János Kádár and Albania's Mehmet Shehu. Cuba responded by restricting U.S. Ambassador Philip Bonsal to Havana's Vedado district as long as Castro's movements were restricted in New York.

Unwelcome at the midtown Shelburne Hotel, Castro and his entourage moved to the Hotel Theresa in Harlem, where he met with Malcolm X, Krushchev, Nasser, Nehru, Kwame Nkrumah of Ghana and black American writer Langston Hughes. During his four-and-a-half-hour speech to the UN General Assembly, Castro denounced UN complicity in the usurpation of power by Colonel Joseph Mobutu (Sese Seko) in the Congo from rightful leader Patrice Lumumba, argued for the inclusion of China in the UN and pledged support for Algerian independence.

The Americans responded with a 10,000-word document repudiating Castro's claim that the U.S. was encouraging unauthorized flights over Cuba. In turn, Cuba filed a formal complaint, accusing the U.S. of aerial aggression.

The U.S. created a partial economic embargo in October of 1960. Fidel Castro was officially an enemy of the United States, but the man most feared by the CIA was Che Guevara. Determined that Cuba must not make the same mistakes Arbenz made in Guatemala, he urged Castro not to be exclusively preoccupied with domestic problems. Without allies, he argued, Cuba could be isolated, as Guatemala had become, and therefore vulnerable.

As well, Che believed that freedom of the press in Guatemala had led to Arbenz's downfall. The independent Cuban newspapers *Prensa Libre*, *El Cristol*, *Havana Post* and *La Calle* all ceased production.

Whereas Castro was attracted to power, Guevara was eager for social change. In this regard, the two men did not clash and often complemented one another. As an ideologue, Guevara was a weathervane for the future of Cuban socialism. Frequently he would make an intemperate remark about domestic or foreign policy, indicating a radical stance, which proved prophetic months or years later. For instance, as early as January and April of 1959, Che had openly discussed the need to nationalize oil and mineral wealth. The CIA and other foreign powers learned to monitor Guevara's statements closely, knowing that Castro was a more careful and clever chess player on the world stage.

If Castro was the king, Guevara was the chief bishop. Eager to export revolution, Guevara had begun to travel extensively as early as June 1959 to seek alliances with non-aligned "third position countries" and emerging states in Africa and Asia. On the home front he was no less active. Interviewed by two Chinese journalists, Guevara indentified the problems of the state.

Guevara said the dictatorial social system and economic foundations had to be abolished; Batista had "cleaned out the national treasury"; an agrarian reform law was required to redistribute ownership of land; racial discrimination persisted; rents had to be lowered.

Divorced from Hilda Gadea on May 22, 1959, Guevara married Aleida March on June 2, 1959. He had dumped the homely Hilda, who had waited for him in Peru with their daughter, in favour of a pretty, young, blond schoolteacher from Santa Clara. As always, he wore his olive green military uniform and his black beret for the wedding. For him, the war was still on. When Castro subsequently urged Che to take his bride with him to Madrid and Cairo, to make a political sojourn into a honeymoon, Che left her behind, arguing that revolutionaries should demonstrate austerity in their personal lives.

As National Bank president he had refused a $1,000-a-month salary. He returned to Cuba in September, having visited 14 countries that included Egypt, India, Yugoslavia, Indonesia, Ceylon, Singapore and Japan.

Influenced by Mao's writings, Che Guevara published his how-to manual, *Guerrilla Warfare,* in 1960, based on his recent experiences. The book was dedicated to Camilo Cienfuegos, the Revolution's most courageous fighter, who was pictured on horseback for the book's cover. Guevara later wrote a memorial tribute to "Camilo, Lord of the Vanguard" in 1964, long after Camilo Cienfuegos had disappeared on a flight from Camaguey to Havana on October 28, 1959.

Despite an extensive search led by Fidel Castro, wreckage of Camilo Cienfuegos's small plane was never found. "This event was also the object of infamous slanders," says Castro.

For decades Cubans surreptitiously suggested Cienfuegos had been eliminated on Castro's orders because he rivalled Castro in popularity. Castro is convinced that mechanical or weather problems were to blame. "All of us here were involved in accidents in airplanes and helicopters during the first years of the Revolution," he says. "I was, Raúl was, several other leaders were. The organization, the measures, the safety there is today for all air travel did not exist at that time."

One of Castro's lovers, an American named Marita Lorenz, claims in her unreliable but provocative 1993 autobiography that CIA operative Frank Sturgis laughingly acknowledged the CIA had killed Cienfuegos. She claims an unnamed CIA agent, on his deathbed, made a similar claim. "Camilo," she writes, "had been killed by the CIA with C-4 plastics used to down his helicopter." In fact, Cienfuegos had left Camaguey in a small plane, not a helicopter.

Given the CIA's abysmal track record at assassination attempts inside Cuba, it's equally plausible that Cienfuegos could have been a victim of the Castro brothers' ruthlessness. The younger Castro resented the far more popular Cienfuegos after Cienfuegos expressed a sympathetic view of a counter-revolutionary insurgency led by Huber Matos in Camaguey in October of 1959, the same month as the plane crash. But an official at the Camaguey airport has reported that Cienfuegos adamantly insisted that his pilot must proceed, even though there was a storm warning. It is most likely that Cienfuegos was the victim of his own brave and impulsive nature as a fearless man who often took chances.

Concerned that more than 80 percent of Castro's troops were illiterate, Che Guevara launched literacy programs at La Cabana fortress with some success. In December 1960 Cuba announced a national literacy campaign to teach reading and writing to approximately one million Cubans.

Prior to the Revolution, according to World Bank statistics, more than half of Cuban children were without any schooling. The comparable figure for Latin America as a whole in 1958 was 36 percent. As touted in the Literacy Museum in Havana, the illiteracy rate for the population reportedly dropped from 25 percent to 3.9 percent after Cuba sent 120,000 literacy workers called *brigadistas* to work throughout the island.

The state's emphasis on education has remained. In the late 1990s the island's literacy rate reached 98.5 percent. School is compulsory to age 15. One out of every 15 citizens is a college graduate. There are four universities. More than 20 medical schools have produced 4,000 new doctors per year. All education is free.

Literacy pamphlet

In 1960, the same year that children helped adults to eradicate illiteracy in Cuba, Castro tried to eradicate Santa Claus. A revolutionary figure called Don Feliciano was invented to replace St. Nick. The American tune "Jingle Bells" was revised with newly sanctioned lyrics, "Jingle bells, jingle bells, always with Fidel."

Relations with the United States had deteriorated rapidly after Castro's visit to New York.

As early as December 11, 1959, the CIA's head of its western hemisphere division, Colonel J. C. King, had sent a memo to CIA director Allen Dulles in which he proposed to "eliminate" Castro. King later confirmed to CIA deputy director of planning Richard Bissell that an assassination might be arranged. By March 1960, the CIA had produced its extensive policy document "A Program of Covert Action Against the Castro Regime." The measures, approved by Washington, included a propaganda offensive, creation of a rival Cuban government in exile, covert actions within Cuba and the creation of paramilitary forces outside Cuba for future guerrilla action.

By March 17, 1960, President Eisenhower had approved CIA plans to train dissident Cuban exiles, chiefly in Guatemala, for a future military incursion.

One of President Eisenhower's final acts as president was to suspend direct diplomatic relations with Cuba on January 3, 1961.

As overt political conflicts increased, covert operations increased. For instance, as revealed by ex-CIA agent Philip Agee, CIA agents placed dynamite in dolls in a Havana department store, with deadly results. Pilots hired by the CIA conducted "softening up" attacks on Cuban defences from Nicaragua, and on April 17 a press release, written by E. Howard Hunt Jr., announced that "Cuban patriots" had begun to liberate Cuba. The CIA's Radio Swan, from a radio transmitter near the Cayman Islands, encouraged Cubans to take up arms against Castro.

This escalation of agitation and violence culminated in the Bay of Pigs invasion, the most humiliating military defeat in United States history.

THE BAY OF PIGS

Just as Batista knew about Castro's plan to invade eastern Cuba in 1956, Castro anticipated the CIA's invasion force.

Cuba's intelligence service had many contacts within the Cuban exile community of Miami. Castro's agents had infiltrated at least one of the seven five-man "Grey Teams" sent by the CIA to coordinate airdrops of weapons and to possibly assassinate Fidel Castro, Raúl Castro and Che Guevara. One of these infiltrators, trained in Guatemala, was a 19-year-old named Félix Rodríguez. He would later change his allegiance and eventually oversee Che's execution in Bolivia six years later on behalf of the CIA.

Castro also suspected an invasion was imminent because President Kennedy had prohibited travel to Cuba by U.S. citizens. More significantly, airfields in southern Cuba were strafed and bombed on April 15, just two days before the invasion. This largely unsuccessful attempt to demobilize Cuban air defence tipped the CIA's hand. Dissidents within Cuba were promptly rounded up by Castro prior to the Bay of Pigs attack. Given enough warning, Castro was able to personally confront the 1,300 mainly Cuban exile soldiers known as Brigade 2506.

There is evidence to suggest Castro knew almost as much about the CIA plans as President Kennedy.

When Colonel Jack Hawkings sent a telegram to Kennedy from the Nicaraguan town of Puerto Cabezas, assuring him everything was going according to plan, Kennedy didn't know internal support for the invasion on Cuban soil had been mostly eliminated. More important, Kennedy didn't even know the Pentagon had assured the CIA that the U.S. president would authorize U.S. military support after the Cuban landing (to avoid the humiliation of any U.S. defeat).

Nicaraguan dictator Luis Somoza provided a cheering farewell to the CIA's Liberation Army from Puerto Cabezas, urging them to bring back a hair from Castro's beard.

They traveled in boats belonging to the United Fruit Company, escorted by U.S. naval destroyers. The leaders of the invasion were the CIA's Grayston Lynch and William (Rip) Robertson, as well as mercenary leader José Pérez San Roman. The CIA had prevented several prominent Cuban exile leaders in Florida, including José Miró Cardona, from participating, much to their lasting resentment.

For their landing site, the CIA had originally favoured the flat southern coast near the city of Trinidad, in central Cuba, but President Kennedy had refused to approve such a "spectacular" location. On April 17, 1961, the mercenaries arrived instead at remote stretches of sand called Playa Girón and Playa Larga in the *Bahia de Cochones* (Bay of Pigs), an area mainly inhabited by very poor charcoal makers.

The CIA hoped its invasionary force could quickly announce the formation of a provisional government, much as Fidel Castro had done, but within 24 hours the invaders were surrounded by 20,000 Cuban troops, led by Castro in a tank and outfitted with Soviet weaponry.

The CIA readied its aircraft on the Zapata Peninsula and the U.S. Navy was offshore. But when General Charles Cabell, the deputy director of the CIA, called Kennedy and asked for back-up, the president wouldn't relent on his position that American forces must not be overtly involved. (Survivors of the botched invasion later testified that CIA advisers at the Trax Base in Guatemala had promised them that their landing force would receive military support. For decades afterwards, right-wing Cuban expatriates blamed President Kennedy for refusing to supply overt U.S. support for the clandestine CIA attack. It is one of the most persuasive rationales to explain John F. Kennedy's assassination in Dallas.)

The CIA had gambled on Kennedy's compliance—and lost.

Two American ships carrying supplies for the invaders, the *Houston* and *Rio Escondidio,* were sunk by propeller-driven Cuban planes. The majority of the CIA's invaders were captured within two days. Castro announced victory after 72 hours. He had lost only 150 men while the *mercenarios* had lost 200 of their number. Eleven hostile planes were shot down, including all the B-26 bombers flown from Nicaragua. According to Cuban authorities, the 1,197 prisoners taken at the Bay of Pigs had previously owned 914,859 acres of Cuban land, 9,666 houses, seventy factories, five mines, two banks and ten sugar mills.

The CIA's director of covert operations, Richard Bissell, contravening Kennedy's command, had allegedly authorized six

U.S. pilots to attack in three bombers equipped with napalm and explosives. This resulted in a public relations coup for Cuba when the body of one of the American pilots was recovered, allowing Castro to prove to the world, and to his people, that American forces had invaded.

In May the Soviet Union awarded Fidel Castro its Lenin Peace Prize, and Castro declared openly, for the first time, that Cuba must develop a socialist constitution. After a tense first meeting with Nikita Khrushchev in June, President Kennedy, doubly embarrassed because the Soviets had launched cosmonaut Yuri Gagarin into space in early April, called for a major increase in American military spending.

"Thank you for Playa Girón," Che Guevara told President Kennedy's aide Richard Goodwin in Uruguay in August. "Before the invasion, the Revolution was shaky. Now it is stronger than ever."

Guevara was at the Punta del Este meeting of the Organization of American States as head of the Cuban delegation. Although the United States was working to ostracize Cuba after the Bay of Pigs fiasco, they would not be able to eliminate Cuba's membership in the OAS for another six months. As a result, the U.S. representative at the Uruguayan conference on Inter-American Economic and Social Conference had to sit through Che Guevara's speech on August 8, 1961.

"What we guarantee," he said, "is not to export revolution. We guarantee that not one rifle will leave Cuba, that not one weapon will go to another country."

The tensions between Washington and Havana continued to escalate.

In 1961 the Cubans planted prickly cactuses along the northeast perimeter of the Guantánamo base to prevent Cubans from fleeing to the American compound. The resulting "no-man's land" became known as the Cactus Curtain.

The Cubans would commemorate their victory at the Bay of Pigs by opening *Museo Girón*. One of the captured Brigade 2506 leaders, Manuel Artime Buesa, confessed on Cuban radio that he had helped to plan the invasion with E. Howard Hunt and Hunt's assistant, Bernard L. Barker, a member of Batista's secret police. This threesome would continue to manage an extensive campaign of armed attacks, sabotage, arson and propaganda from the University of Miami, code-named JM WAVE, after Buesa's release.

Castro offered to exchange the Bay of Pigs prisoners for political prisoners held by CIA-supported regimes. Kennedy refused. Castro then offered to free them in exchange for 500 bulldozers, but Kennedy was willing to supply only 500 tractors. In the end, most of the prisoners were not released until December of 1962, approximately twenty months after the invasion, in exchange for $53 million worth of medical supplies and baby food. Nine prisoners were retained. The final Bay of Pigs prisoner wasn't freed until 1986.

THE KENNEDY ERA AND THE MISSILE CRISIS

The Bay of Pigs defeat called for revenge. The United States had been humiliated. The Kennedy manhood was challenged in the process. Reconciliation with Fidel Castro and the radical likes of Che Guevara, who dubbed America "the most barbarous nation on earth" in 1960, was not in the cards.

In November President Kennedy designated his brother, Attorney-General Robert Kennedy, as the commander of Operation Mongoose, a new plan to overthrow Castro with a $50-million-a-year budget.

President Kennedy fired the men chiefly responsible for the Bay of Pigs invasion, CIA director Allen Dulles, and his top associates Charles Cabell and Richard Bissell.

In December Kennedy continued the suspension of Cuba's sugar quota, and in January the U.S. successfully encouraged the Organization of American States to expel Cuba on the grounds that its adherence to Marxist-Leninism was "incompatible with the inter-American system." The OAS also voted to suspend all weapons sales to Cuba.

In February Kennedy tightened trade restrictions, banning all exports to Cuba except medical supplies. In April the U.S. rehearsed an invasion of Cuba by mounting "Operation Quick Kick" on the Puerto Rican coast, assembling 83 warships, 300 airplanes and 40,000 men.

A psychological propaganda campaign called "Operation Peter Pan" was developed as an adjunct to Operation Mongoose. It included the circulation of a rumour in Cuba that parents would lose their paternity rights to the state and some Cuban children would be sent to Siberia. The head of the Catholic Services Bureau of Florida, Monsignor Walsh, subsequently reported that some 15,000 children left Cuba without their parents between December 1960 and October 1962.

The U.S. floated plastic bags to Cuba containing propaganda and chewing gum, dropped American flags and children's toys decorated with propaganda and distributed five million comic books containing caricatures of Fidel Castro. The heightening of tension only solidified Castro's resolve. "I am a Marxist-Leninist," he declared, "and I shall be a Marxist-Leninist to the end of my life."

Cuba asked for a meeting of the UN Security Council to discuss American aggression and formally protested repeated provocations by American soldiers at Guantánamo. As a goodwill gesture, Cuba also released 60 wounded Bay of Pigs prisoners in April.

Forced to introduce rationing of foodstuffs and basic supplies, Cuba simultaneously introduced an ambitious polio vaccination campaign. Polio was eradicated from the island, earning Cuba a citation from the World Health Organization for its pioneering efforts.

Having become president of the United States in early 1961, John F. Kennedy had to take some steps to appease the Cuban exile community. In Miami there were 400 CIA case officials who monitored and controlled thousands of Cuban agents and contacts, with hundreds of millions of dollars at their disposal to foment unrest. On May 12, a Cuban patrol boat was attacked at sea. Three Cubans were killed and five others were wounded.

In response to American aggression, Nikita Khrushchev subsequently met with his newly appointed ambassador to Cuba, Alexandr Alexiev, and asked him if he thought Fidel Castro would accept the presence of Soviet nuclear rockets in Cuba.

This was the germination point for the Cuban Missile Crisis.

A former KGB agent and Spanish Civil War veteran, Alexandr Alexiev had arrived in Havana on October 1, 1959, and become friendly with Che Guevara. He told Khrushchev that Castro was unlikely to accept the offer. Having rid the island of American military advisers, he argued, Castro couldn't appear to compromise Cuban sovereignty.

Khrushchev imagined a different scenario. He suggested Castro wouldn't have much choice in the matter. According to Khrushchev, Americans only understood force. That was why the United States were deploying nuclear-tipped Jupiter missiles pointing at the USSR from Turkey. These NATO deployments, negotiated in 1959 by the outgoing Eisenhower administration, didn't please Kennedy, but he had assented for domestic reasons, not wanting to antagonize the Pentagon.

"We can give them back the same medicine they gave us in Turkey," Khrushchev told his ambassador. "Kennedy is pragmatic, he is an intellectual. He'll comprehend and won't go to war, because war is war. Our gesture is intended to avoid war, because any idiot can start one but we're not doing that, it's just to frighten them a bit. They should be made to feel the same way we do. They have to swallow the pill like we swallowed the Turkish one."

Khrushchev's plans had almost as much to do with China as the United States. Chinese communists were increasingly unwilling to be subservient to the Soviet Union. They were also critical of Khruschchev because he was abandoning the ideal of revolution in favour of Soviet prosperity. The Russian leader was therefore under pressure to reassert his dominance as the world's foremost communist leader.

"Khrushchev's one great asset," wrote British historian Edward Crankshaw, "which he exploited unremittingly, was universal fear of nuclear war." Fear-mongering could be as effective as warmongering.

In the face of mounting incursions under the umbrella of Operation Mongoose, Fidel Castro met with a Soviet delegation and agreed, in response to their hypothetical question, that threat of war with the Soviet Union would serve the United States as a strong disincentive to attack Cuba. The Soviets suggested installation of 42 medium-range missiles, 36 of which would be operational.

Castro requested time to consider the proposal. His decision to accept Khrushchev's plan to secretly install nuclear missiles was made on May 30, 1962, in consultation with Raúl Castro, Che Guevara and several others. As Minister of the Armed Forces, Raúl Castro signed an agreement in Moscow in early July with the Soviet defence minister. The missile sites were installed within 76 days of Fidel Castro's acceptance.

The first nuclear warheads arrived on a Soviet freighter on October 4, 1962. Estimates of the strength of the Soviet forces and the number of nuclear warheads differ. Soviets have claimed there were 43,000 military personnel; American estimates are higher. Some sources claim 20 warheads were turned back by the blockade and none of the sites were fully operational during the crisis.

According to the Rio de Janeiro Treaty of 1947, Cuba had a right to obtain and install defensive weapons if Cuba was not threatening peace in the Caribbean. As well, Cuban leaders understood that, in accordance with Operation Mongoose, Cuba would likely be invaded by the United States in October. In the preceding month Air Force Chief of Staff Curtis LeMay had received a plan for the aerial bombardment of Cuba to precede the invasion of U.S. troops. When U-2 aerial photographs confirmed on October 14 that the Soviet Union was construct-ing missile sites, American plans to attack Cuba were put on hold. The intimidation plan appeared to be working.

As a chess player, Khrushchev was winning the game. His audacious gambit had halted American aggression.

Speaking on national television on October 22, President Kennedy warned that nuclear war was imminent. "It shall be the policy of this nation," he said, "to regard any nuclear missile launched from Cuba as an attack by the Soviet Union on the United States, requiring full retaliatory response on the Soviet Union."

The fate of Cuba was now entwined with the fate of the world. World War III was a doomsday script that only required one impulsive move to become reality.

On October 22, President Kennedy shifted the U.S. military from Defense Condition 5 to DefCon 3. As Kennedy addressed the nation, the U.S. ordered 54 Strategic Air Command bombers into the air and prepared 136 Atlas and Titan ICBM missiles for firing. Polaris submarines were sent to stop Soviet vessels on their way to Cuba.

The missile sites were controlled by Moscow, not Cuba. The ensuing crisis was a posturing drama between Kennedy and Khrushchev, with Castro in the middle, relatively powerless.

By October 24, the U.S. had instigated a naval blockade around the island. Privately Kennedy feared that if Americans tried to take Havana, Khrushchev could take Berlin. For the first time in history—but not the last—the U.S. military was placed on a DefCon 2 alert.

To begin the tense bargaining process, Khrushchev wrote two letters to Kennedy without consulting the Cubans. He asked the U.S. to end the blockade, to promise not to invade Cuba and to remove its nuclear weapons from Turkey. In return Khrushchev promised not to interfere in Turkish affairs. But Khrushchev and Kennedy were not the only players in the deadly game.

Thomas Powers, commander of the Strategic Air Command, and U.S. Air Force Chief of Staff Curtis LeMay were urging Kennedy to bomb Cuba on the grounds that Russia wouldn't dare respond because the American arsenal was far superior. On October 26, Powers ordered an unsanctioned launch of an ICBM from Vandenburg Air Force Base across the Pacific. This missile reached its intended target, the U.S. missile testing range in Kwajalein atoll in the Marshall Islands, to demonstrate American military prowess.

This rogue firing of the American missile was tantamount to a shot across the bow, a taunt at Russia as the inferior military power, a deliberate provocation.

On October 27 a U.S. spy plane was shot down over Cuba, supposedly by a Soviet commander. According to Carlos Franquí, the editor of Cuba's *Revolución*, Fidel Castro was directly responsible. While Castro was touring one of the Russian rocket bases, a U-2 spy plane appeared on the radar screen and he asked how the plane could be shot down. According to Franquí, the cocksure Castro impulsively pushed the button he was shown. "Fidel pushed it and the rocket brought down the U.S. plane. Anderson, the American pilot, was the only casualty in that war. The Russians were flabbergasted." Castro has denied this story.

Also on October 27 Kennedy formally asked the Soviet Union to withdraw its missiles from Cuba in return for an end to the blockade and his promise not to invade Cuba. Privately, unbeknownst to the American public, Attorney-General Robert Kennedy met with Soviet Ambassador Anatoly Dobrynin and promised the U.S. would withdraw its Jupiter missiles from Turkey.

When an agreement was reached on October 28, the Soviets began to dismantle their nuclear sites without consulting Castro.

As Robert Kennedy had promised, NATO missiles were removed from Turkey by April 1963. That same month, when Castro went to the Soviet Union and visited Khrushchev outside Moscow, the Soviet leader read Kennedy's correspondence to him. The American president wrote, "We have complied with all of our commitments. We withdrew the missiles from Italy and Turkey."

It was the first time Castro had heard Italy mentioned in the deal.

After the missile crisis, in the year preceding Kennedy's assassination, relations between Cuba and the United States remained adversarial. Cuba made demands that Cuban airspace mustn't be violated, that the Americans should rescind Guantánamo Bay and that subversive activities inside Cuba should cease. "The naval base has only served to offend the honour of our nation," Castro has said. Cuba rejected American and Soviet plans to allow for inspection of their military sites. Castro argued, logically, that the American pledge not to invade should not be grounds for an exchange of access.

"The United States has no right to invade Cuba," he said, "and we cannot negotiate on the basis of a promise that a crime will not be committed."

The American naval quarantine or blockade was lifted on November 20 after Kennedy had received assurances from Moscow that Soviet IL-28 bombers would be withdrawn. The Americans officially dismantled Operation Mongoose in January of 1963.

In June new plans were made for covert operations to destroy Cuban oil refineries, power plants and a major sugar mill. As the president who had resolved in 1962 to withdraw American troops from Vietnam, John Kennedy had to maintain some appearances of a hawkish stance towards Cuba to mollify right-wing American interests.

John and Robert Kennedy had already alienated conservative white Americans by advancing the civil rights movement for blacks. To be seen to be soft on Cuba was risky. Nevertheless the American president spoke frankly in October 1963 with French journalist Jean Daniel.

"I believe that there is no other country, including those in Africa and others under colonial domination, where there has been more humiliation and exploitation than Cuba," Kennedy said, "in part attributable to the policies of my country during the Batista regime. I believe that we contributed to creating and building the Cuban movement, in spite of the form it took.

"I can assure you that I understand the Cubans. I approved of the proclamation that Fidel Castro made in the Sierra Maestra when he called for justice and the liberation of Cuba from corruption."

Jean Daniel, whose interview with Kennedy appeared in the *New Republic*, went to Cuba and interviewed Fidel Castro. He asked Castro whether he thought Americans were justified in fearing Cuba's communist affiliation with the Soviet Union.

"Asking me to say that I am not a piece of the Soviet chess game," Castro replied, "is the same as asking a woman to shout in public that she is not a prostitute."

Two days later in Jean Daniel's presence, upon learning of Kennedy's assassination, Castro repeatedly said, *"Es una mala noticia."* This is bad news.

The "bad news" for Fidel Castro would continue throughout the presidencies of Johnson, Nixon, Ford, Reagan, Bush and Clinton. Looking towards his election, President Lyndon Johnson informed his staff that he didn't want to appear tolerant of Cuba. When West German Chancellor Ludwig Erhard visited the White House that December, Johnson persuaded him to join an economic embargo against Cuba.

Only President Jimmy Carter would show signs of refusing to kow-tow to anti-Castro sentiments generated by the American militia and the Cuban exile community. Carter would briefly re-establish diplomatic relations in 1977. He would also encourage

a Treasury Department ruling to allow Americans to vacation in
Cuba without entering via Mexico or Canada, as well as permit
Americans to spend American dollars in Cuba. These reprieves
would be short-lived.

4 | MODERN TIMES

Havana taxi driver trying to make a living from tourism

Coming so soon after the Kennedy assassination, the bizarre assassination of Lee Harvey Oswald by Jack Ruby—captured on film while Oswald was being held in the custody of Dallas police—was not seriously questioned by the American public.

During their time of grief, the American public was spared the news that Jack Ruby was a close and notorious affiliate of the Trafficante syndicate, a prominent Mafia force in Cuba during Batista's reign. American media easily persuaded the American people that Lee Harvey Oswald, Kennedy's alleged lone assassin, was most likely an agent of communism.

Throughout his presidency Lyndon Johnson maintained a tough, anti-Cuba stance in public and put direct pressure on other countries, such as Britain and Spain, not to trade with Cuba. Even though the United States would trade with the Soviet Union, it would not cooperate with Cuba.

MARXIST-LENINISM BY DEFAULT

Inaugurated as president in 1969, Richard Nixon had political debts to some of America's most powerful corporations. These companies wanted to regain their former holdings in Cuba. As well, Nixon's close friend and golfing partner, Cuban-born Charles G. "Bebe" Rebozo, who had his own suite in the White House, was a direct link to anti-Castro ex-Cubans in Miami. Fidel Castro had nowhere to turn but to the Left.

Increasingly isolated, Castro's government demanded Cubans contribute in a massive effort to produce a record 10-million-ton sugar harvest in 1970. Compulsory military service amounted to free labour, and to desert a plantation could result in five to thirty years in jail.

"The situation was almost intolerable," Reinaldo Arenas

recalled. "Unless you have lived through it, you could not possibly understand what it means to be in a Cuban sugar plantation under the noon sun, and to live in barracks like slaves. And this was happening in the country proclaiming itself the First Free Territory of the Americas."

The grandiose sugar initiative strained resources and morale. Cuba fell short of the 10-million-ton quota. In a speech made on the anniversary of his Moncada Barracks attack, Castro admitted the sugar initiative had seriously disrupted Cuba's progress in other economic sectors. He offered to resign, whereupon the crowd rejected this option for him. It was a classic Castro ploy, turning a national failure into grounds for a personal endorsement.

In 1964 Castro had gone to Moscow and negotiated sales of sugar to the Soviet Union, at prices in Cuba's favour—two million tons in 1965, three million in 1966, four million in 1967 and five million annually until 1970. With the record production of 8.5 million tons in 1970, Cuba still couldn't evolve beyond its dependency on Soviet aid.

Russian became Cuba's second language, Soviet technology began to transform Cuba's infrastructure and housing, and Cuba pledged its solidarity with non-aligned states and anti-American countries such as Vietnam, Laos and Cambodia. Castro became a significant ally of Salvador Allende in Chile.

On a 63-day tour in 1972 Castro made diplomatic and practical connections with Eastern Europe and several small African nations: Equatorial Guinea, Mauritania, Sierre Leone, Somalia, South Yemen and Zambia. Cuba soon befriended Algeria and Tanzania, and supported lengthy dictatorships in Gabon and Zaire. Most significantly, Castro provided lasting support, military aid and Cuban soldiers to Angola in the 1970s and 1980s.

Castro criticized the brutal American-supported puppet regimes in Central America, particularly Guatemala, where horrific torture and genocide were rampant, and he provided assistance for the leftist Nicaraguan government of Daniel Ortega and the Sandinistas. He increasingly became a thorn in the side of the United States, supporting American dissidents such as Angela Davis and providing sanctuary for members of radical groups such as the FLQ in Canada.

The establishment of a classless society—in theory, at least—was made a formal government objective. Many apolitical Cubans, loyal in their hearts to Cuba, were unwilling to embrace Marxist-Leninism and defected to the United States. All Cubans who traitorously embraced the United States were vilified by Castro's regime as "worms."

The Cuban Revolution still had the broad support of the populace. Having made public health a priority for more than a decade, in 1973 Cuba was able to announce that it had achieved the lowest infant mortality, 28.7 per 1,000 live births, in Latin America. Cuba would eventually boast a better infant mortality rate than the United States. In 1974 Cuba created the most progressive maternity laws in the world, providing working women with six weeks off work before birth and three months afterwards, plus guaranteed time off for prenatal care and pediatric visits. In 1975 Cuba's Family Code was enacted to guarantee equality between men and women.

In 1976, marking the twentieth anniversary of the landing of the *Granma,* Castro announced he would transfer the "emergency powers" of his revolutionary government to a National Assembly. Also in 1976, Cuba was divided into fourteen provinces instead of six. A new constitution was introduced to allow for local elections, but these structural changes to create

Poder Popular (Popular Power), as an attempt to obviate criticism abroad, had minimal impact on the status quo within the country because the Popular Power still resided with Fidel and was managed by an elite.

"We consider the construction of socialism as a transition period in which one class is prevalent over the others—the dictatorship of the military," Castro explained. But his rule remained highly personal and absolute. He has been called the "Saddam Hussein in the Caribbean" and his government has been variously described as "romantic paternalism," "scientific caudilloism" and "charismatic hardship communism."

The first mass rebellion by the Cuban populace occurred in 1980. In April a bus driver drove his passengers through the gates of the Peruvian embassy. They all asked for political asylum. When the Peruvian ambassador asserted international law and protected the dissidents, Castro removed the military guard around the embassy. This was an error in judgment. By the time the embassy doors were closed a day later, approximately 10,800 Cubans had flocked into the embassy compound and thousands more were waiting outside.

In his anger, Castro decided to allow malcontents—including criminals, homosexuals and mental patients—to leave the island. The situation backfired for Castro when tens of thousands of Cubans made their way to the coastal town of Mariel, eager for exile. This exodus was largely financed by Cuban exiles and became known as the Mariel boatlift. Hundreds of privately owned boats sailed from Florida to assist the would-be emigrants. The Mariel Freedom Flotilla brought 125,000 Cubans to Key West (90 miles away) and Miami (250 miles away).

The Mariel boatlift encouraged more *balseros* (rafters) to attempt the crossing, mainly from the coast between Havana and

Matanzas. It's a journey that can take anywhere from a few hours to several weeks, depending on winds, currents and modes of transportation. According to a United Nations estimate, one-fourth of all *balseros* don't survive the windy, shark-infested waters, often dying of thirst. Those who are captured or turn back receive severe jail sentences. Despite the dangers, the influx of Cuban refugees after 1980 became so burdensome that in 1994 the United States reversed its 1966 Cuban Adjustment Act in order to stop the deluge of rafters.

Since 1959 more than one million Cubans have left the island, either legally or illegally. During this time the person who was most able to consistently challenge Castro's authority was Celia Sánchez. Fidel Castro's 23-year relationship with her ended with her death from cancer in 1980. Afterwards Castro allocated considerable resources for cancer research, hoping to honour the memory of Celia Sánchez with a medical discovery on par with her impotance to Cuba, and to him. (Cubans are justifiably proud that a Cuban doctor named Carlos Juan Finlay discovered in 1881 that malaria is transferred by a certain type of mosquito.)

A political argument is easily made that Cuba's Revolution lost

Fidel Castro and Celia Sánchez

its momentum in 1989 when the Soviet Union withdrew its economic support. Russian oil exports to Cuba dropped from 13 million tons to six million tons, literally leaving millions of Cubans in the dark and reliant on a million Flying Pigeon bicycles from China instead of automobiles. Also in 1989, on July 13, a firing squad eliminated the charismatic war hero Arnaldo Ochoa. Castro had framed the disaffected and vocal Ochoa, who had led Cuban troops in Angola, Nicaragua and Ethiopia (and had considerable prestige within the armed forces as a result), for drug trafficking. Castro watched the replay of the execution on videotape.

But a psychological argument might be made that the Cuban Revolution lost its soul and became a mere dictatorship when Fidel Castro lost his personal compass, Celia Sánchez. It is rumoured that Castro has maintained Celia Sánchez's apartment as a personal shrine and sometimes goes there to think and to sleep.

Although he is never seen in public with a woman, Fidel Castro has never lacked for female companionship. Some of his sexual companions have offered unflattering views—he didn't take his boots off, he read while making love, he talked too much, he was hasty—but he maintained a lasting relationship with Delia Soto del Valle Jorge, "the Trinidad woman."

Similar to Naty Revuelta, Delia Soto was a green-eyed, light-skinned beauty from a well-to-do family. As his mistress she bore him five sons in the 1970s—Alex, Alexander, Alejandro, Antonio and Angelito. Four of them have Castro's middle name Alejandro somewhere in their own name; all were partially educated in the Soviet Union. As well, Castro has another illegitimate son, Jorge Angel, by a woman known only as Amparo, and he allegedly fathered a son by his first American mistress, Marita Lorenz.

Fidel Castro has been a father figure for all Cubans, but only eight of his offspring are acknowledged as his. Once depicted on a billboard as one of the Three Wise Men, Fidel Castro takes a paternalistic attitude to the population while simultaneously insisting he has consciously restricted the development of any "cult of personality." This stated aversion to a "cult of personality" means Castro's birthplace in Birán, El Turquino and his La Plata command headquarters in the Sierra Maestra are all kept off-limits to tourists and Cubans alike, accessible only through complicated screening procedures.

THE DESPERATE NINETIES

In 1991 Nelson Mandela visited Cuba to thank Cubans for their role in undermining apartheid in South Africa. Mandela acknowledged with gratitude that Castro's steadfast military support of leftist liberation in Angola had significantly countered the military power of the white apartheid regime in South Africa. Castro had stationed as many as 50,000 Cuban troops in Angola, fortifying the black resistance movements throughout southern Africa in the process, until their withdrawal in December of 1988.

In 1977 Cuba had also sent 17,000 troops to Ethiopia, at the request of the Soviet Union, to counter a U.S.-backed insurgency movement from Somalia. But the deadly Angolan campaign, resulting in more than 2,000 Cuban fatalities, had proved very unpopular within Cuban homes, not unlike the Vietnam War in the United States.

Despite severe economic difficulties, Havana successfully hosted the 1991 Pan American Games at which Cuba won 140 gold medals and the United States 130 gold medals. But no amount of athletic prowess, or praise from Nelson Mandela, could compensate for losing Cuba's $6-billion subsidy in oil, food, technology and military aid from the Soviet Union. Near the close of 1991 the Soviet Union withdrew 11,000 military and technical personnel from Cuba.

With the collapse of the Soviet Union, Castro could only retrench Marxism in Cuba with austerity programs that brought resentment. Without Soviet support, Cuba stagnated. "It's like history's on the pause button here," says a character in Pico Iyer's novel *Cuba and the Night.* "Everywhere else in the world, everything's either on fast-forward or rewind. This is the only place I know where everything's moving and nothing ever changes."

Russian embassy

In September of 1992 Fidel Castro admitted to the Cuban people that Cuba's purchasing power had fallen from $8.1 billion in 1989 to $2.2 billion. In 1992 the gasoline ration for cars was cut to three U.S. quarts a month. The monthly state ration was reduced to five pounds of rice, four pounds of sugar, one pound of beans, 16 eggs, 12 ounces of chicken, four ounces of coffee and precious little oil, garlic and soy.

In the same year, the United States passed the Torricelli Act, which prevented foreign subsidies of American corporations from trading with Cuba. In addition, any ships from any country that had entered Cuban ports were prevented from entering any U.S. ports for at least six months.

America was putting on the squeeze.

Arguably the beginning of the end, in terms of the degradation of state socialism, was February 1, 1993. On that day a Cuban newpaper called *Trabajadores,* meaning Workers, carried an item about Cuban workers serving the tourist industry in Varadero, the beach resort town that increasingly catered to foreigners. Whereas Cuban waiters, chambermaids and bellhops, etc., had previously pooled their tips in dollars and exchanged those tips for pesos that were divided equally between them, a new policy henceforth permitted individual workers to keep their tips in American dollars.

For Marxism in Cuba it was like a leak in a dam that couldn't be plugged. Faced with a growing black market economy, Castro relented and accepted the American dollar as an alternate currency. On June 15, 1993, Cuban officials at a business conference in Cancún announced that Cuban citizens would be allowed to possess American dollars. Castro elaborated on this change on July 26 on the fortieth anniversary of his Moncada attack, by citing Cuba's dwindling economy. By September Castro had legalized self-employment in more than 100 trades. Private enterprise was back. By the fall of 1994 it was legal for all Cubans to possess American dollars.

Castro was forced to develop tourism with international partners. Whereas in the 1960s and early 1970s, Cuba had attracted approximately 3,000 visitors a year, 1993 saw 600,000 tourists. The government set a target of two million tourists for the year 2000. As Christopher Columbus had once reported to his patrons, Queen Isabella and King Ferdinand, "Where there is such marvellous scenery, there must be much from which profit can be made."

Cuban citizens were no longer permitted unfettered access to the upscale hotel zone of Varadero, where the old Dupont mansion, Xanadu, caters to sightseers as an expensive restaurant and an adjoining golf course caters to the elite.

Economic apartheid produced predictable results. Prostitution, the scourge of Havana under Batista, made a strong comeback, informally at first. Young, self-confident and beautiful women known as *jineteras,* female jockeys, cruised the streets and the countryside, hoping to earn more in one night than a secretary might earn in a year. Their male equivalents, *jineteros,* aggressively pestered tourists to buy cigars, accept rides in illegal taxis or accept their offers to procure female companionship. Although Cubans were outlawed from the hotel rooms of tourists, bribes could be paid to hotel staff when necessary.

For many Cubans, the average monthly wage in pesos was worth about $10 in U.S. currency. In a society where physicians earned only 500 to 600 pesos a month, doctors chose to work as waiters. The infiltration of the American dollar was undermining Cuban society far more effectively than all the clumsy and violent efforts of the CIA. Even Cubans began to openly assert that the Marxist Revolution could not continue without Fidel Castro.

Behaviour changed with expectations. The dogmatism of Fidel Castro was tolerated rather than revered. For many young people it became more important to "get ahead," to buy a television set, to marry a tourist, than to serve the goals of Castro's admirable but doomed social experiment. A few might brazenly refer to Fidel Castro as *El Loco.* Older Cubans refused to believe that Fidel Castro was committing "suicide by tourism," trusting that *El Líder* would eventually solve Cuba's latest social and economic crisis.

Castro had once decreed that Marxist-Leninism was "just as Cuban as palm trees." But his leadership was more in keeping with the Spanish tradition of *caudillismo,* the authoritarian rule of strongmen. This syndrome had been foreseen by the great liberator Simón Bolívar, who recognized *caudillismo* as inevitable and necessary for effective governance in Latin America. "Many tyrants will arise upon my tomb," he said prior to his death in 1830.

After more than 40 years of one-man rule in Cuba, it became necessary to wonder if Fidel Castro's approach to government wasn't a copy of the management approach of his father, Angel Castro, who effectively operated the family farm and plantations with absolute authority. Often Cuba seemed less like a country and more like Castro's family farm, a fiefdom in which he would not tolerate or excuse any opposition.

Critics of Castro like to assert that nearly half the Cuban work force in the 1990s is unemployed, homosexuals have been persecuted and many Cubans survive on "a miserable 1,400 calories per day." Freedom of the press in Cuba was strictly curtailed soon after Castro took control. *Plantados* (dissidents) incarcerated in penitentiaries and psychiatric hospitals are often abused, as described in Armando Valladeras's memoir of his 22 years in jail, *Against All Hope*. The Cuban penal code allows for anyone who is disrespectful of authority to be punished by jail terms.

Anyone who might have rivalled Castro in terms of charisma is either dead or disgraced. The heroic deceased comrades include Frank País, Camilo Cienfuegos and Che Guevara. More recently eliminated rivals include Huber Matos (democrat, sentenced to 20 years in prison), Humberto Sorí Marín (economist, executed with multiple bullets to the head), Heberto Padillo (independent writer, arrested, beaten, forced to recant, disgraced), Angola war hero Arnaldo Ochoa (executed on drug charges), Radio Rebelde founder and former editor of *Revolución* Carlos Franquí (expunged from official photos and self-exiled to France) and the brilliant dissident writer Guillermo Cabrera Infante (living abroad since 1962).

"Freedom was something constantly talked about but not practiced," recalls Reinaldo Arenas. "There was freedom to say that there was freedom or to praise the regime, but never to criticize it."

For his part, Castro rejects the argument that Cuba is a dictatorship. He contends that, like the pope, he is duly elected by fellow authorities in order to serve and honour Marxist-Leninist principles. He also asserts that he is a dedicated consensualist. "All my life," he told Nicaraguan Sandinista leader Tomás Borge, "right from the beginning, I have promoted group decisions—never one-person decisions. I've had a very clear, very precise understanding of this, and it has protected me against what might be called any form of absolute power."

An argument that Marxist-Leninism is culturally inappropriate for Latin Americans has been advanced. "They're treating Marx the way the Southern Baptists treat the Bible," complains the narrator in *Cuba and the Night*. "I mean, here you are, you've got a funky tropical island in the Caribbean, hot, spicy, all sex and rum and colour, and you try to get it to dance to some ideas laid down by a nineteenth-century German in the British Museum. Might as well tell the Brits to go Rasta."

A visit by Castro's fellow patriarch Pope John Paul II in 1998 was orchestrated to improve Castro's image, but unfortunately the Bill Clinton–Monica Lewinsky scandal in the United States grabbed the headlines in North America. Nonetheless world opinion shifted even more strongly against the Helms-Burton Act, engineered

Pope John Paul II

by Senator Jesse Helms and Indiana Republican Dan Burton to punish any companies that did business with Cuba.

President Clinton had approved sanctions after Cuba's air force shot down four Cuban exile pilots, three of them U.S. citizens, at the edge of Cuban airspace in February 1996. This pivotal confrontation—possibly approved by Castro in order to halt the trend towards normalization of relations—derailed Congressman Bill Richardson's talks in Havana, begun in 1995, to ease sanctions.

Since 1992 the United Nations had voted overwhelmingly in favour of a resolution that called for the U.S. to end its trade embargo. By 1995 only three countries had opposed the motion—the United States, Israel and Uzbekistan. But in 1995 the U.S. Congress strengthened Cuban trade restrictions and the House rejected, by a vote of 283 to 138, an amendment from Washington State Democrat Jim McDermott to exempt sales of medicine and food.

In return for his access to Cuba and millions of lapsed Catholics, the pope spoke against the Helms-Burton Act. "Restrictive measures imposed from outside the country are unjust and ethically unacceptable," he said. The pope's first address was made, incongruously, in Santa Clara, on a sports field near the hills where Che Guevara had overcome Batista's soldiers and scored a major victory to free Cuba from capitalism (and Catholicism). From Havana Fidel Castro scratched the pope's back in return. "I am moved by Your Holiness's efforts on behalf of a more just world."

Republican John Warner of Virginia subsequently led a call to have Congress and the White House review and revise U.S. policy towards Cuba. "We allow food and medicine to go into Iraq," he said, "and we deny this tiny country basic things."

Responding to criticism from conservatives such as Warner and the pope, Secretary of State Madeleine Albright suggested some restrictions might be eased regarding mail, money and travel. But in essence the White House under Clinton failed to act.

In 1998 the United Nations again voted on a motion that called on the United States to lift its punitive embargo—a wide-ranging embargo likened to a medieval siege. There were only two dissenting votes, those cast by the United States and Israel.

In spite of increasing pressure from U.S. business interests to re-open Cuba for U.S investment, the embargo remained in effect throughout President Clinton's two terms in the Oval Office.

On January 1, 1999, to mark the fortieth anniversary of the Revolution, Fidel Castro returned to the square in Santiago de Cuba where he had pronounced victory. Forty years before, flushed with victory and vindication, he had declared, "I am not interested in power nor do I envisage assuming it at any time." This time he spoke for 90 minutes to a relatively small crowd that included Nobel literature laureates Gabriel Garcia Márquez of Colombia and José Saramago of Portugal.

While the ultra-conservative *Forbes* magazine had identified Castro as one of the richest rulers on the planet, with a personal worth estimated at $100 million, Castro stubbornly decried the international role of financial speculators who "have turned the planet into a giant casino."

Castro, the man increasingly seen as "the Last Communist," once more predicted the capitalist system would fail, but this time he also recognized that seven million of Cuba's eleven million people had been born after the Revolution. "The people I lead," he noted ruefully, "are not the same people of that January first."

Neither was the Cuban economy the same. By century's end, Cuba had lost its traditional position as the world's leading sugar producer. Unemployment was growing drastically and the population was increasingly malnourished.

Social unrest increased. Amnesty International filed extensive reports of hundreds of incidents in which Cuban authorities stifled dissent, frequently imprisoning intellectuals and journalists. There was an alarming increase in the persecution of individuals who attempted to exercise free speech in the late 1990s. In 1999 the Cuban National Assembly passed legislation that approved setting prison terms of up to 20 years for Cubans seen to be "collaborating" with the U.S. government's policies towards Cuba.

As crime escalated, changes to the penal code introduced the death penalty for some drug-trafficking offences as well as life sentences for major crimes. In a five-hour speech to 5,000 police officers in January of 1999, Castro frankly admitted crime and violence were both on the rise. He said more than 1,200 Cubans were arrested in 1998 for drug offences. In the previous year, several thousand prostitutes had been rounded up, but with minimal impact. The population's growing reliance on foreign currency, chiefly American dollars, was resulting in a crisis of moral values.

"There are even irresponsible families who sell their daughters' bodies and insensitive neighbours who think this is the most natural thing in the world," Castro said, "until tragedy and disease strike."

As Cuban society became more fractured and unstable, the country's once-charismatic leader was looking more like a reclusive Howard Hughes than an unstoppable Che Guevara. In November 1999 Fidel Castro considered visiting Seattle during the World Trade Organization's summit to lobby for the withdrawal of the U.S trade sanctions. He decided at the eleventh hour to forgo the attempt.

Although the future of communism under Fidel Castro appears limited, given his age, he will never admit defeat. Novelist Pico Iyer has noted that for 40 years Fidel Castro has not changed his uniform or his hairstyle. "The other one-name icons—Madonna and Prince and Cher—had at least to keep changing their acts to keep themselves in the public eye: not Fidel," writes Iyer. "He just fixed the public's eye to keep it on himself."

By 2000 the Republic of Cuba under Castro had outlasted the Soviet Union by nine years, and with George W. Bush gaining power in 2001, Castro had matched wits—easily—with nine American presidents.

EPILOGUE

Europeans imagined an earthly paradise across the Atlantic Ocean long before Christopher Columbus was born. A fourteenth-century English poem referred to this imaginary paradise as "Cockaygne"; the Spanish called it El Dorado.

Cuba still has the makings of that earthly paradise.

Cuba is an island with an ideal climate and has largely overcome a degrading legacy of slavery. Its leader is more intelligent than almost any other leader; its people are humorous, cooperative, well-educated, inventive and healthy. But Cuba's persistence in the modern era has not been appreciated by those who govern the world's most powerful nation.

Four and a half centuries of colonialism and exploitive capitalism gave rise to Fidel Castro, the *líder máximo*. Whether or not he remains in power, or whether he is alive or dead, it is impossible not to admire the spirit of Cubans in the shadow of the United States. And if you go there, it is impossible not to feel enduring sympathy for their struggles.

5 | DICTATORSHIP INDEX

Fidel Castro and Yasser Arafat visiting the Moncada Museum

THE FOLLOWING ARE SOME dictators, despots and kings who have lived since 1950 and the approximate number of years of their *unelected* power as of 2001.

Kim Il Sung (1912–94) North Korea: 46

King Hussein (1935–99) Jordan: 46

Emperor Haile Selassie (1892–1975) Ethiopia: 44

FIDEL CASTRO (1926–) Cuba: 42 *

Enver Hoxha (1909–85) Albania: 41

King Hassan II (1929–99) Morocco: 38

Francisco Franco (1892–1975) Spain: 36

António de Oliveira Salazar (1889–1970) Portugal: 36

Josip Broz Tito (1892–1980) Yugoslavia: 35

General Alfredo Stroessner (1912–) Paraguay: 35

Sultan Muda Hassanai Bolkiah (1946–) Brunei: 33 *

Mobutu Sese Seko (1930–97) Republic of Congo/Zaire: 32

Muammar Qudhafi (1942–) Libya: 32 *

Joseph Stalin (1879–1953) Soviet Union: 31

General Suharto (1921–) Indonesia: 31

Rafael Trujillo Molina (1891–1961) Dominican Republic: 31

Zayed bin Sultan al-Nuhayyan (1918–) UAE (Abu Dhabi): 30 *

Hafez al-Assad (1928–2000) Syria: 30

King Jigme Singye Wangchuck (1955–) Bhutan: 29 *

Dr. Hastings Kamuza Banda (1898–1997) Malawi: 28

Mao Tse-tung (1893–1976) China: 27

Chiang Kai-shek (1887–1975) Taiwan: 25

Moussa Traoré (1936–) Mali: 23

Daniel arap Moi (1924–) Kenya: 23 *

Nicolae Ceausescu (1918–89) Romania: 22

Muhammad Siad Barre (1919–95) Somalia: 22

Saddam Hussein (1937–) Iraq: 22 *

Julius Kambarage Nyerere (1922–99) Tanzania: 20
"Ne Win" or Maung Shu Maung (1911–) Burma: 19
King Fahd bin Abdulaziz Alsaud (1923–) Saudi Arabia: 19 *
Gamal Abdal Nasser (1918–70) Egypt: 18
Augusto Pinochet (1915–) Chile: 17
Mengistu Haile Miriam (1974–91) Ethiopia: 17
Gaafar Muhammad al Nimeiry (1930–) Sudan: 16 *
Anastasio Somoza Garcia (1896–1956) Nicaragua: 16
Jean-Claude "Baby Doc" Duvalier (1953–) Haiti: 15
Ho Chi Minh (1890–1969) North Vietnam: 15
Ferdinand Edralin Marcos (1917–89) Philippines: 14
Francois Tombalbaye (1918–75) Chad: 13
Omar Torrijos Herrara (1929–81) Panama: 13
King Farouk I (1936–52) Egypt: 12
Nikita Sergeyevich Khrushchev (1894–1971) Soviet Union: 11
Leonid Ilyich Brezhnev (1906–82) Soviet Union: 11
Fulgencio Batista y Zaldívar (1901–73) Cuba: 11
Mohammad Zia ul-Haq (1924–88) Pakistan: 10
Samuel Kanyon Doe (1951–90) Liberia: 10
Ayatollah Ruhollah Khomeini (1902–89) Iran: 10
Michel Micombero (1940–83) Burundi: 10
Achmad Sukarno (1901–70) Indonesia: 10
Juan Domingo Peron (1895–1974) Argentina: 9
Idi Amin (1925–) Uganda: 8
Ramiz Alia (1925–) Albania: 7
Sani Abacha (1943–98) Nigeria: 5
Manuel Antonio Noriega (1934–) Panama: 5
Pol Pot (1928–98) Cambodia: 4

* Still in power. Years of non-democratic power are approximations as of 2001. Queen Elizabeth is excluded because she has no real political power.

INTO THE TWENTY-FIRST CENTURY

By 2001 the United States was reportedly the third largest source of visitors for Cuba's $2 billion tourist industry after Canada and Germany. Thousands of American tourists were defying the U.S. travel ban, flying from countries such as Mexico, Canada or Jamaica.

The U.S. House of Representatives voted in July 2001 to lift the travel ban, but President Bush stopped its passage into law. President Clinton's administration had recently been soft on the Cuba issue, relinquishing the motherless rafter Elian Gonzalez to his father in Cuba.

In 2000 Russian President Vladimir Putin visited Cuba and reiterated the importance of the island's spy centre at Lourdes, built by the Russians in 1964 as an electronic eavesdropping centre for monitoring the U.S. In October 2001, Putin closed the base to save the Russian military $200 million a year and to enhance his relations with the U.S. following the terrorist attacks on New York City and Washington.

Fidel Castro took ill for the first time in public on June 23, 2001, while addressing 60,000 people for two hours in Havana. Castro's far less popular brother Raúl has been touted as a possible successor, but there are at least four other candidates. Ricardo Alarcón has experience as president of the People's National Assembly, speaks English well and served in the underground during the Revolution. Dr. Carlos Lage has led Cuba's economy into the new century, having devised plans in 1991 for Cuba's "mixed enterprises" with foreign capital. Felipe Pérez Rogue and Hassan Pérez are two younger possibilities. Rogue has been Cuba's foreign minister and Pérez, a former president of the University Students Federation, has delivered some of Fidel's speeches for him.

6 | THE DEATH OF CHE GUEVARA

A Cuban postcard: Che Guevara playing a final round of golf (with Fidel Castro) at the Havana Country Club prior to the demolition of Cuba's golf courses

Visiting Cuba in 1960 with Simone de Beauvoir, Jean-Paul Sartre met Che Guevara and later described him as "the most complete human being of our age."

Apparently the great French philosopher failed to notice that Che Guevara was murderous, lacking in compassion, self-absorbed, stubborn, dirty, contemptuous of women, vengeful, uncompromising and vain.

For several years after the Revolution, Che Guevara worked tirelessly to mould the new state of Cuba. He was the model for the "New Man." A cult of Che worship arose during his lifetime in response to his rhetoric, his successes in guerrilla warfare and his handsome face.

Guevara's mystique as a Marxist hero increased when he eschewed family life and comfort in order to foment revolution in poor countries. In Cuba he effectively replaced Jesus. "Be like Che," schoolchildren were told.

Che Guevara addressed the United Nations in 1964, then traveled to Algeria where he was interviewed by Josie Fanon, widow of Frantz Fanon, author of *The Wretched of the Earth*. Prior to disappearing from the public eye in March of 1965, Guevara also visited Mali, Congo (Brazzavillle), Ghana, Dahomey, Tanzania and the United Arab Republic.

As the greatest twentieth-century revolutionary of the Western Hemisphere, he had yet to assuage his ego.

Che Guevara left Havana on April 1, 1965, disguised as a clean-shaven businessman named Ramón Benítez. He arrived in Dar-Es-Salaam on April 19 via Moscow and Cairo, determined to do for millions of Africans what he and Fidel Castro had done for Cubans.

On April 24 he left behind the safety of Tanzania to participate in the Congolese rebel forces of Laurent Kabila. Guevara and a handful of intensely loyal Cuban cadres arrived unannounced, assuming Guevara would be welcome to engage in the military planning and fighting.

The disorganized rebel forces in Africa proved to be frustrating allies. After a series of setbacks, Guevara left the Congo on November 28. In one version of his Congolese memoirs he frankly wrote, "This is the story of a failure." But Guevara maintained his unwavering resolve in public, writing from Africa in 1965, "There is no life outside the revolution."

Che Guevara in disguise

While cloistered in secrecy and mainly determined to write, Guevara had a six-week reunion with his wife Aleida in Dar-Es-Salaam in January and February. "It was the first time we had ever been alone together," she said. In March he took refuge in a safe house on the outskirts of Prague, then he secretly returned to Cuba, at the urging of Castro, to a safe house on the eastern edge of Havana.

Guevara didn't want to return to Cuba less than a hero. On October 3 of the preceding year, with Guevara's wife and children present, Fidel Castro had read aloud to the nation the text of Guevara's "farewell letter" to Fidel Castro and Cuba. "I feel I have fulfilled the part of my duty that tied me to the Cuban Revolution in its territory," Guevara stated, "and I say good-bye to you, the comrades, your people, who are already mine." At the time a renowned Egyptian journalist named Hamdi Fouad asked

Che's wife why she was dressed in black at the time; Aleida replied, "Because he is going to die."

With Africa proving too problematic, Guevara was determined to kindle revolution throughout Latin America instead. He hid in Cuba and planned his next move with Fidel Castro.

Che Guevara's ultimate goal was to "liberate" his homeland, Argentina. In order to do so, he would have to enter Argentina from a neighbouring country such as Bolivia. Preliminary meetings were held with potential allies such as Bolivian Communist Party Secretary-General Mario Monje. He advised Fidel Castro that an armed guerrilla insurrection in Bolivia was not realistic.

Peru was arguably a more fertile breeding ground for revolution. Bolivia was less than ideal for two reasons: agrarian reforms to ameliorate the peasantry had recently been introduced there, and factional disputes and jealousies between Monje's communists and Bolivian Maoists were growing. This factionalism would prove deadly.

Despite Monje's advice, Castro instructed him to prepare a rebel initiative for Guevara east of Sucre. (Debate persists as to whether this choice of Bolivia was Castro's or Guevara's. "It would appear," writes Guevara expert Jon Lee Anderson, "that it was Fidel himself who persuaded Che to start the struggle in Bolivia, sometime in the spring of 1966.")

In 1966 Guevara tested a new identity. His new appearance as a balding businessman with black glasses was so convincing that Castro's closest advisers didn't recognize him. But Che Guevara wasn't the first revolutionary to infiltrate Bolivia in disguise. The "deep-cover" courier known as Tania had gone ahead to La Paz in 1964 posing as an attractive Argentinian ethnologist named Laura Gutiérrez Bauer. Some of her other aliases were Lary Aguilera, María Aguilera, Elma, Najda and "T."

Tania was, in fact, Haydée Tamara Bunke Bider. Born in Argentina in 1933, she was the daughter of Jewish communists who had fled Hitler's Germany in 1931. When she was 14, her family moved to the German Democratic Republic, and at 18 she joined the youth wing of the Communist Party. Working as a Spanish/German interpreter, she

Tania

first met Che Guevara in Berlin in early 1961. It is widely believed that they became lovers near the outset of their relationship. She moved to Cuba later that year. An ardent communist, she soon received permission to wear a Cuban military uniform.

In Bolivia Tania found a volunteer job, befriended the Bolivian president's press secretary and married an unsuspecting Bolivian engineer in order to gain Bolivian citizenship. An attractive Slavic woman given to writing melancholy poetry, she remained true to her mission. She dispensed advice to the lovelorn on a Bolivian radio station, sending coded messages to Havana in the process, and eventually made the arrangements to establish Che Guevara's base camp at remote Nancahuazú.

On November 3, 1966, Che Guevara arrived in La Paz posing as a Uruguayan economist on a fact-finding trip for the Organization of American States. As "Aldolfo Mena González," he photographed himself in the mirror of his suite in the Hotel Copacabana.

"I've come to stay," he told his companions on their way to their guerrilla base camp at Nancahuazú, "and the only way that I will leave here is dead."

In Nancahuazú Guevara met with emissaries from Peru and Argentina, but he failed to heal the rifts among Bolivian leftists. At the end of 1966 Mario Monje traveled across the Bolivian Andes to discuss the situation, but he found Guevara unwilling to consider any compromise to his complete control. The Cubans wanted the Bolivian communists to follow Havana and not Moscow; Monje left Nancahuazú and never spoke with Guevara again.

At his crude headquarters Guevara also had meetings with French journalist Régis Debray, as arranged by Tania. On their way to Nancahuazú, the scrupulously efficient Tania had atypically left four incriminating notebooks in a locked Jeep parked on the street. Debray and the Argentinian leftist Roberto Ciro Bustos had cautioned Tania about her decision to do so. The police in the town of Camiri subsequently confiscated these documents from the Jeep, thereby gaining an extensive list of contacts and funding sources. This strange event raised Debray's suspicions about where Tania's deepest loyalties lay.

Born in 1941, Régis Debray first visited Cuba as a philosophy graduate student in 1961. Impressed by Castro's Marxist tendencies and by Guevara's literacy campaign, he became a leading proponent of the Cuban Revolution. Following his travels in South America, he published his Marxist analysis of Latin America in Jean-Paul Sartre's review. Returning to Cuba to teach philosophy at the University of Havana, he spent time with Fidel Castro and published *Revolution in the Revolution?* in January of 1967. Debray, codenamed "Dantón," arrived in Bolivia with credentials to write for a Mexican weekly. Traveling under his real name, he also wrote for a French publisher before joining Che Guevara in Nancahuazú.

Having lost the confidence of Bolivia's top communists, Guevara was trying to mount a guerrilla crusade with limited success. In his revolutionary force, besides Tania and himself, were 29 Bolivians, 16 Cubans and three Peruvians. The logistics of supplies, transportation and communication proved insurmountable. Their situation grew desperate when Castro inexplicably stopped re-supplying Guevara in March 1967.

In their disastrous nine months of rebel activity, solidarity was strained and Guevara was seriously ill much of the time. He soiled himself and was frequently unable to walk. Desperately short of food, his men sometimes had to kill their mules or horses in order to eat. Looking like desperadoes, the revolutionaries frightened the local peasantry.

Before his departure from Havana, Che Guevara had urged comrades to create "two, three, many Vietnams." They were not able to create one.

As a courier for the Cubans, Régis Debray was captured and interrogated by Bolivian authorities after the Bolivians had outlawed the Communist Party and declared a state of emergency in the country's southeastern region.

It was Régis Debray who confirmed Guevara's presence in Bolivia in April of 1967. Debray was sentenced to 30 years' imprisonment for abetting the insurrectionists, but due to international pressure from the likes of Charles de Gaulle, he was released in 1970. (The following year Debray, disillusioned with Castro, told French intellectual André Malraux that Guevara's mission had failed partly because Tania was a Soviet agent whose loyalties were primarily to Moscow, not Havana. Former East

German intelligence officer Gunter Mannel has confirmed Tania's KGB connections.)

When it was learned that Guevara hadn't died in the Congo, the CIA sent American Special Forces "Green Berets" to Bolivia to prepare a counter-insurgency team called the Rangers.

"Tania the Guerrilla" was killed by Bolivian soldiers in an ambush at Masicurí on August 31, 1967. The so-called "Vado del Yeso" massacre, overseen by Captain Mario Vargas Salinas, reduced Che Guevara's force by one-third. This victory boosted the morale of the Bolivian military. There were parades and visits to the army headquarters at Vallegrande by President René Barrientos, his top generals and their wives.

On September 8 the body of Tania, the only female insurgent, was brought to the hospital in Vallegrande. Her body was blackened and mutilated because she had been swept downstream and not found until several days after the massacre. An ardent non-believer, she was ironically accorded the honour of Christian last rites by the personal order of President Barrientos. The man who undertook the secret burial of Tamara Bunke, Lieutenant Colonel Andrés Selich, had buried Tania's comrades a few days before. He retained one of Tania's romantic poems for posterity.

After a series of clashes, setbacks and retreats, Che Guevara was pinned down in a ravine, at an elevation of 6,500 feet, on October 8. His force reduced to 17 men, Guevara was wounded by a bullet in the calf of his left leg. Out of ammunition, Guevara tried to escape after an afternoon gunfight. He was confronted in the bushes by an Indian sergeant named Bernardino Huanca.

"Don't shoot," Huanca was told. "I am Che Guevara. I am worth more to you alive than dead."

Huanca's superior, Captain Gary Prado Salmon, soon appeared and confirmed Che Guevara's identity. Lieutenant Colonel André Selich, as Captain Prado's superior in nearby Vallegrande, was notified immediately by helicopter. Che Guevara and a fellow prisoner were taken to the remote hamlet of La Higuera.

That night Che Guevara lay on the dirt floor of a mud-walled schoolhouse, bound hand and foot, alongside the bodies of two fallen comrades, while the Bolivia high command considered its next move.

The following morning a helicopter arrived at 6:15 a.m. carrying Colonel Joaquin Zenteno Anaya and the CIA agent known as "Captain Ramos." Ramos was Cuban exile Félix Rodríguez, who had been captured at the Bay of Pigs invasion. He'd been with the CIA's Miami operations following his return from Nicaragua in 1964. Rodriguez had been asked to volunteer for the Bolivian assignment in June and he had eagerly complied. According to Rodríguez, who took photographs that day, Guevara was oozing blood "like a piece of trash," without proper footwear, emaciated, with matted hair.

The CIA wanted Rodríguez to evacuate the haggard prisoner to Panama; Lieutenant Selich agreed that Guevara should be kept alive as a propaganda tool. Some of Guevara's fellow prisoners were executed in the morning while Selich and Rodríguez waited for "higher-ups" in La Paz to determine Guevara's fate.

While Che Guevara waited, he asked to see the local schoolteacher, Julia Cortéz, age 22. She nervously approached the stranger. He looked like a trapped animal, not a man. He motioned to the blackboard and pointed out a grammatical error. He informed her the squalidness of her school was disgraceful and by Cuban standards it would be considered on par with a prison.

When Che Guevara asked to see Julia Cortéz a second time that day, she was too intimidated and didn't go back to the school.

At 12:30 p.m. Colonel Zenteno Anaya received a radio message on behalf of President Barrientos and his chiefs of staff. (Rodríguez has claimed that *he* received this coded radio message, not Zenteno.) Zenteno was told to "eliminate" Guevara. Colonel Zenteno refused to disobey a direct order from La Paz.

Not eager to play the role of executioner directly, both Lieutenant Colonel Selich and Colonel Zenteno left La Higuera in the helicopter. They conferred the dubious honour of murdering Che Guevara on Lieutenant Colonel Miguel Ayoroa, who was in charge of the unit that had captured him.

The CIA's Félix Rodríguez had to decide whether he could risk removing Guevara from Colonel Ayoroa, essentially kidnapping the prized prisoner from the Bolivians. He decided the risk was too great. With much reluctance, Félix Rodríguez informed his nemesis, Che Guevara, he would die.

"It's better like this," Che told him. "I never should have been captured alive. Tell Fidel that he will soon see a triumphant revolution in America. And tell my wife to remarry and try to be happy."

Rodríguez embraced Guevara. "It was a tremendously emotional moment for me," he recalled. "I no longer hated him. His moment of truth had come, and he was conducting himself like a man."

(The Bolivian helicopter pilot who took Che's corpse from La Higuera, Nino de Guzman, told the Associated Press in 1998 that Che Guevara repeatedly said, "Fidel betrayed me." Retired Air Force General Nino de Guzman claims he gave Guevara some tobacco. "I was probably the last person to talk at length with Che before he was executed," he says.)

Wearing a Bolivian army uniform, Félix Rodríguez had his photograph taken standing alongside Che Guevara outside the schoolhouse. It was the last known photograph of Che Guevara alive.

Lieutenant Colonel Ayoroa had asked for volunteers to kill Guevara. He selected a short sergeant who had lost three comrades during the gunfights of the previous day. This man was Mario Terán.

Félix Rodríguez asked Mario Terán to shoot Che Guevara in the face; that way it might look as if Guevara had died from wounds suffered during a battle. "I walked up the hill and began making notes," Rodríguez recalled. "When I heard the shots I checked my watch."

Che Guevara was killed by Mario Terán at 1:10 p.m. He used a semiautomatic rifle, first hitting Guevara in the arms and legs. While Guevara writhed on the ground, Terán fired another blast, this one into Guevara's thorax. His asthmatic lungs filled with blood, bringing death, on October 9, 1967.

He was 39 years old.

Che Guevara's body was tied to a stretcher, secured to the landing skids of Nino de Guzman's helicopter and airlifted to the nearby town of Vallegrande.

(Nino de Guzman took photos of Guevara's corpse before it was cleaned up for the Bolivian press. These photos were reportedly passed along to the Associated Press in 1998. It is conceivable that Nino de Guzman's version of events is meant to discredit Fidel Castro, because he contends that Che Guevara questioned Cuba's decision to incite revolution in Bolivia instead of Peru. Captain Gary Prado Salmon has also claimed Guevara told him the decision to come to Bolivia was Castro's.)

Mario Terán kept Che's pipe, Zenteno kept his damaged rifle. Selich kept one of Che's several Rolex watches, as did Captain Gary Prado and Rodríguez. Before disappearing from Vallegrande, Rodríguez also took Che's last pouch of tobacco. He stored it inside the butt of his favourite revolver upon his return to the United States.

The corpse had to be cleaned up before it was presented to the press for posterity. The nun who washed his body remarked that Che Guevara resembled Jesus Christ, as did other nuns in the hospital. This impression spread throughout the town. Some of the women in Vallegrande came to the hospital and snipped bits of Guevara's hair.

The body was placed on public display atop a concrete wash-basin in the laundry house behind Vallegrande's Nuestro Señor de Malta Hospital. The press and public paraded past the corpse, but Havana would not immediately accept the news of Che Guevara's death. To convince Castro and the world, General Alfredo Ovando Candía suggested beheading the corpse, keeping the head for evidence. Rodríguez suggested chopping off one finger.

A compromise was struck. Guevara's hands were amputated. His hands were preserved in jars of formaldehyde for Argentinian forensic experts. The handless body was buried surreptitiously early on October 11 near the Vallegrande airstrip, under the direction of Lieutenant Colonel Selich. Six of Guevara's comrades were also buried in a mass grave.

Three Cubans miraculously evaded capture. Three months later Harry "Pombo" Villegas, Dariel Alarcón and Leonardo "Urbano" Tamayo made their way to the Andes and were rescued by Chilean socialists. Senator Salvador Allende, a future victim of the CIA, flew with this trio to Easter Island. They eventually returned to Cuba via Tahiti, Ethiopia, Paris and Moscow.

In 1995 retired Bolivian General Mario Vargas Salinas—who had had a photograph taken of himself standing alongside Che Guevara's corpse—tried to cooperate in locating Che Guevara's grave. Excavations were unsuccessful. At last the remains of Che Guevara were recovered on June 18, 1997, by a team of Cuban and Argentinian scientists. The identity of "Skeleton #2" was easily confirmed because it had no hands. As well, the scientists found remains of an olive army jacket like the one Guevara was wearing when he was shot.

The remains were flown back to Cuba and entombed in a grand, new Soviet-style memorial at Santa Clara, the city where Guevara had led a famous military victory on December 29, 1958. Santa Clara was also the city where Aleida March, his second wife, had been a schoolteacher before her relationship with Guevara.

The remains of Tania were unearthed a year later. They were found approximately half a mile from Guevara's grave in Vallegrande. (Jon Lee Anderson's invaluable biography, written with assistance from Guevara's widow, Aleida March, doesn't provide any mention of the possibility that Che Guevara and Tania had been lovers. It is generally assumed they were.)

The bones of Cuba's second-most-famous female revolutionary—after Celia Sánchez—were interred within the Che Guevara mausoleum in Santa Clara in a ceremony to coincide with the fortieth anniversary of the Cuban Revolution. The headquarters of the Federation of Cuban Women, in a converted Vedado mansion in Havana, also celebrates Tania with a mural alongside a mural of Che Guevara.

Che Guevara lives on, more famous in death than in life.

"Che" banknotes honoured him as The Heroic Guerrilla. There have been countless Che stamps, Che billboards and Che paraphernalia. Within Cuba his image is inescapable; there are framed Che photos in nearly every home.

Outside Cuba Che Guevara is an icon almost as recognizable as Andy Warhol's Campbell Soup can. His visage is no longer merely political. Che is a ubiquitous marketing device for T-shirts, websites and key chains. An episode of *The Simpsons* TV program included a Latin nightclub called Chez Guevara. A political thriller by John Blackthorn called *I, Che Guevara,* imagines what would happen if Guevara was not really killed in Bolivia and had returned in 1999 to once more affect Cuba's future. He remains as the Eiffel Tower of revolutionary chic. The only people in twentieth-century history who might be more widely recognized in the year 2000 are Hitler, Madonna, Mao, Einstein, JFK, Princess Diana and Michael Jordan. Che Guevara belongs in the top 10 of contemporary fame, alongside Gandhi, alongside Stalin, alongside Churchill, as Latin America's second most famous twentieth-century personality.

The most famous image of Che Guevara is a black-and-white photograph that shows Che wearing a black beret with one star on it. This picture was taken in 1960 when Alberto "Korda" Gutierrez was a staff photographer for *Revolución,* a Cuban newspaper.

Gutierrez was covering a memorial gathering in Havana for the 136 men who died in the March 4 explosion of a French freighter, the *Coubre,* which was bringing arms and munitions from Belgium. (Belgium had ignored a request from the United States to stop supplying arms to Cuba.) Also in attendance were Jean-Paul Sartre and Simone de Beauvoir.

Che Guevara briefly appeared on the stage. In the wake of the Revolution, it was dangerous for Castro and Guevara to make themselves available as targets for snipers. That day Fidel Castro was delivering another of his long speeches. Gutierrez was able to take only two photographs of Guevara before he disappeared again.

Gutierrez liked one of those two pictures. He enlarged it and kept it on the wall of his studio. It was never seen in the pages of *Revolución*.

Seven years later an Italian arrived in his studio with a letter of introduction from a high-ranking Cuban communist official. This man wanted a copy of the best image of Che Guevara that Gutierrez could provide. The next day the Italian returned and received two copies of the image that was on the studio wall.

There was no charge. If the Italian was a friend of the Revolution, Gutierrez was pleased to be of service.

Gutierrez only later learned his visitor was the famous Italian publisher Giangiacomo Feltrinelli, the man responsible for smuggling the manuscript of Boris Pasternak's *Doctor Zhivago* out of the Soviet Union.

Feltrinelli was an opportunist. He had come to Havana from Bolivia where he had been helping to negotiate the release of Régis Debray, the French Marxist. While in Bolivia, Feltrinelli had learned that Che Guevara and his guerrillas were having severe difficulties. He understood it was only a matter of time before Che would be captured or killed. He anticipated that Che Guevara would become a "hot property" if he became a martyr for Marxism.

Feltrinelli claimed copyright of the photograph. It shows a dashing, brooding and determined Che wearing his beret and gazing into the future. This image, taken and enlarged by

Gutierrez, has been widely circulated, making Che Guevara the unofficial poster boy for revolution.

The Christ-like image of Guevara's corpse, although it appeared in many underground newspapers and left-wing publications, is not the sort of thing to hang up on one's bedroom wall.

Cuba is not a signatory of the Berne Convention on copyright. Fidel Castro once contended that protection of intellectual copyright is imperialistic "bullshit." Hence the image of Che Guevara fell into the public domain.

Millions of Che posters later, in the late 1990s, the United Kingdom Churches in Advertising Network was looking for a way to update the public's perception of Jesus. Working with an agency called Christians in Media, British men of God were trying to make Jesus Christ more hip.

"We want people to realize that Jesus is not a wimp in a white nightie or someone who is a bit of a walkover," said Reverend Tom Ambrose, "but a strong revolutionary."

With a crown of thorns instead of a beret, the modern black-and-white image of Jesus on the poster that was distributed by thousands of U.K. churches in 1998 was deliberately familiar. It's a direct ripoff of the photo hurriedly taken by Gutierrez in 1960.

Gutierrez died of a heart attack in Paris while visiting an exhibition of his work in May 2001.

7 | THE ASSASSINATION FILE

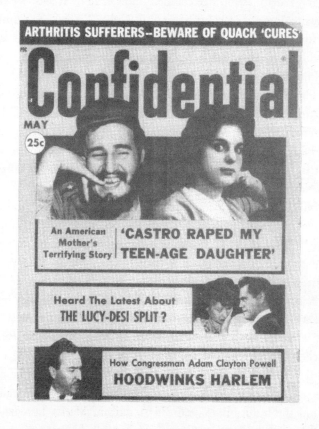

American tabloid from the 1960s linking Fidel Castro and Marita Lorenz

I've spent a lot of time in the Ministry of the Interior's files doing research on the plots against Fidel over the past 35 years," says General Fabián Escalante, Castro's former head of state security. "We have documentation of 612 of them, but I think there were even more."

As part of a CBS television special about the CIA (June 10, 1977), Fidel Castro once claimed knowledge of at least 24 CIA assassination plots on his life within Cuba. "When the number of times I could have been killed are considered," Castro has said, "it does seem that luck has played an important role."

Luck and love.

The most remarkable assassination attempt on the life of Fidel Castro is described in the 1993 autobiography of Castro's first American mistress, Marita Lorenz. Her story became the basis for a Lifetime Movie-of-the-Week presentation, *My Little Assassin,* starring Joe Mantegna as Castro and Gabrielle Anwar as Lorenz, on November 20, 1999.

Nicknamed "Alemana Fria" by the CIA, the German-born Lorenz fell into a twisted, brainwashed double life after falling in love with Castro in 1959. All of her story might not be true, but that certainly doesn't make it entirely false. Marita Lorenz is a witness to history whose story cannot be easily dismissed.

According to Lorenz's memoir, Fidel Castro was living on the twenty-third floor of the Havana Hilton Hotel on February 27, 1959, when he saw a German cruise ship, the M.S. *Berlin,* docked in the harbour. Curious, Fidel Castro and 20 bearded soldiers pulled alongside the luxurious vessel in a small launch. He wanted to see German engineering at close range; instead he found the beautiful 19-year-old American, Marita Lorenz, the daughter of the captain, Captain Heinrich F. Lorenz.

Her father was taking his regular afternoon nap so she claims she took control. She demanded Fidel Castro and his men disarm before they set foot on German territory. They did. The friction became flirtation immediately.

Despite the language barrier, he learned that the M.S. *Berlin* was on its last stop during a two-month Caribbean tour. Marita was born in Germany, but her mother was an American. Traveling in close quarters inside the elevator on their way to inspect the engines, Castro put his arm around her. She didn't object.

Castro talked and drank with Marita's father, a former Nazi, for most of the afternoon. He offered Captain Lorenz the position of Cuban ambassador of tourism, but the man declined. After dinner, it was time to say good-bye. On deck, Castro took Marita between two lifeboats and kissed her. It was her first kiss. (According to her autobiography, Lorenz had been raped by an American sergeant in post-war Germany at age seven. He was court-martialled at the U.S. naval compound at Bremerhaven, Germany and sentenced to 99 years in prison.)

The M.S. *Berlin* was sailing in a matter of hours. The newly installed head of Cuba pleaded with her to stay. He gave her one of his gold watches as a present to remember him by. *"Prometa,"* he said. Promise.

Back at home in New York, Marita received a welcome telephone call. Could she come to Cuba? Fidel asked. Her father lived in Germany; her mother was away. In less than 24 hours, Marita Lorenz impulsively accompanied three of Castro's aides to Idlewild Airport.

Marita Lorenz took up residence in Suite 2406–8 of the Havana Hilton. Tonka toys, records, money and paper were spread about the room. There was a bazooka under the bed. They made love frequently. It was a bachelor's pad. A week later Castro gave her a diamond engagement ring with an 18-karat-gold setting.

He gave her the rank of lieutenant, a .38-calibre revolver and her own honorary July 26 uniform. Isolated at the epicentre of Castro's regime, she helped to translate Castro's "History Will Absolve Me" into English. Her presence was accepted in varying degrees by the vanguard of the Revolution on the top floors of the Hilton—Che Guevara, Raúl Castro, Celia Sánchez, Ramíro Valdés and Camilo Cienfuegos.

Pregnant with Castro's baby, Marita suffered severe morning sickness and became withdrawn. The relationship was now problematic for Castro, who had a new regime to create and manage. As well, there were lots of other female admirers asking for his time, including Ava Gardner.

Marita claims she traveled with him to New York, Washington and Boston, remaining hidden in hotel rooms while Fidel Castro enjoyed the attention of the media. "I am like Jesus, don't you think?" he joked. "I have a beard, I am 33 years old, and I am like God!"

Back in Havana, she read his fan mail from women, seething with jealousy. She claims Ava Gardner once slapped her in the face. Their baby was due in December. Noticeably pregnant, Marita acted as his translator when Castro met the Mafia to decide the fate of casinos. At the time she repeated her father's advice to Castro—don't alienate the Americans.

On October 15, while Castro was away in a different part of Cuba, her room service meal was allegedly drugged. In a stupor, she was taken out of the hotel, injected with more drugs, and her labour was induced. When Marita revived back in her hotel room, she was bleeding profusely.

Camilo Cienfuegos saved her life. He stopped the haemor-rhaging, cleaned her up, sent for antibiotics, nursed her and contacted Fidel Castro, who was furious about the abduction.

Cienfuegos called Marita's brother in New York. It was hurriedly decided that she should be airlifted to the United States to receive the best possible medical attention.

Returning to the U.S., she insisted on wearing her bloodied lieutenant's uniform. She was anemic, suffering from septicemia and had a D&C to stop the bleeding at Roosevelt Hospital. Soon afterwards American secret service agents somehow produced glossy, four-by-five photos of an infant boy's mutilated corpse. It was shown on a bedspread like the one in Fidel Castro's room at the Hilton. This was ostensible proof that Castro had killed her baby.

While Lorenz was reeling from these events, one of Castro's aides infiltrated the hospital and assured her the baby was alive. He passed along the message that Fidel Castro loved her.

Meanwhile, her mother was helping FBI agents convince her daughter that Castro was a baby killer. Born Alice June Lofland, her mother was a privileged cousin of Henry Cabot Lodge and had endured extreme privations during World War II as an American woman living in Germany with her children. Returning to the United States, she had begun working for the U.S. National Security Agency.

American doctors told Marita she could never have another child. As well, for propaganda purposes, Castro was sent a bill for the operation at the Roosevelt Hospital, and Marita's mother filed a lawsuit against the Cuban government for $11 million. The tabloid magazine *Confidential* prepared an exposé, FIDEL CASTRO RAPED MY TEEN-AGE DAUGHTER, to be bylined by Marita's mother.

Castro sent Marita a telegram. She went to a pay phone and called him back. On his private line he reiterated that their baby was fine. The doctor responsible for drugging her and inducing her labour had been shot. It was all a nightmarish plot by his many enemies. He asked her to return to Havana.

In December the CIA sent her back to the Havana Hilton for a two-day visit. They wanted to know how Fidel Castro would react to her presence. Castro told her that children in Cuba belonged to the father, and she could only have her baby if she returned to Cuba.

Marita Lorenz returned to New York without any proof that her baby was alive. To escape the forthcoming *Confidential* article, she went to Germany to visit her father, but the contents of the *Confidential* article were reprinted on the front page of *Stern* magazine.

There was no way of escaping her past and there was no way of understanding it either. FBI and CIA agents urged her to seek revenge on Fidel by murdering him at the same time as she fraternized with pro-Castro groups who recognized her as Fidel's common-law wife.

During this period of confused loyalties, she claims Mafia leaders told her they'd give her $6 million if she killed Castro. Brainwashed into complicity, Marita Lorenz agreed to fly back to Havana from Miami on Cubana Airlines to kill her lover.

The CIA gave her two deadly pills to do the job. Nervous during the 30-minute flight, she took the pills from a special pocket in her slacks, wrapped them in tissue, and hid them in a jar of Ponds Cold Cream. Upon landing and going to the Hotel Colina to quickly change, she discovered the pills had gone soft and mushy in the cold cream.

Dismayed, she went down to the street in her lieutenant's uniform. She easily hailed a ride to the Hilton Hotel in an army Jeep, because anyone in a revolutionary army uniform could use an army vehicle as a taxi.

She went to Fidel's room. Her key still worked. The room was a mess as usual. She couldn't find signs of other women and felt relieved. She took out the pills. Her hands were shaking. Cleaning off the cold cream, she dropped one of the pills into the toilet. Agitated, she threw out the other sodden pill and flushed.

Fidel entered, tired.

"Did they send you to kill me?" he asked.

Marita said yes. Fidel Castro lay down on the bed. He took a .45 revolver from a gun belt hanging over a lamp and handed it to her, butt first. It was the gun he had carried throughout the Revolution.

She pressed the release, removing the ammunition.

"Nobody can kill me," he said.

As arrogant as ever.

"I will kill for the baby," she replied.

But Marita Lorenz was still in love with him. She reached for his boots and untied the laces. She noticed he was wearing different-coloured socks as usual. She noticed his teeth had been fixed. Fidel drank a Coke; she had a *café con leche*. He patted the bed and she lay down.

They made love again. Marita got on her knees and begged to see their son. He told her she would have to return to live with them in Cuba.

Back in the bathroom she discovered the pills were still floating in the bowl. She flushed again. The best chance the CIA had to kill Fidel Castro went down the toilet.

When Castro left the Hilton to make a television address, Marita wrote a letter to her son and another letter to Castro, then left him all but $50 of the $6,000 the CIA had given her for her trip. Back on the street, agents from CIA's Operation 40 were irate that she had given that "commie bastard" Castro $6,000 to "get herself laid."

The CIA escorted her back to José Martí airport. But the story didn't end there.

Marita Lorenz remained a turbulent tragedy of operatic proportions. She had an illegitimate daughter by the deposed Venezuela dictator General Marcos Pérez Jiménez. Then she ran guns for the CIA. Next she drove to Dallas on a covert mission with Operation 40's Frank Sturgis and six others, including a man called "Ozzie," whom she remembered clearly as a skinny and out-of-shape guy she'd met on training sessions in the Everglades. "He couldn't carry or lift anything, or participate in any of the training exercises. He gave me the creeps."

It was November 1963. The skinny guy was Lee Harvey Oswald. In Dallas Lorenz claims she saw E. Howard Hunt give Frank Sturgis an envelope filled with money. Later that same night she met a "mob guy" who was middle-aged, of medium build, wearing a hat. "Hey, what's that goddam broad doing here?" the hoodlum said. "I don't do business with broads." This was Jack Ruby.

Peeved by Jack Ruby's attitude towards her and the "creepiness" of Ozzie, Marita left Dallas before JFK was shot. A few months later she was told to leave the country by two Immigration and Naturalization agents.

Earlier, when it seemed apparent that Venezuelan ex-dictator Marcos Pérez Jiménez would be extradited to Venezuela, he had convinced her to launch a paternity suit to keep him in the United States. This action failed, Marcos was deported and she earned the enmity of Attorney-General Robert Kennedy for her efforts. No longer welcome in America, she flew to Caracas with her daughter and found Marcos in prison.

In Caracas Lorenz was imprisoned herself, separated from their daughter, Monica, and interrogated. She relived painful memories of being stuck in an SS children's home inside the Belsen concentration camp during World War II. After nine days in the Caracas jail, she and Monica were taken in a four-seater Cessna to go "sight-seeing."

They were dropped at Ciudad Bolívar, the last airstrip on the Orinoco River. Three weeks later the same pilot returned. This time he deposited them at a remote settlement of naked Yanomano Indians. During her eight months in the Venezuelan jungle she contracted malaria, settled into jungle life and enjoyed unashamed sex with a Yanomano man named Katcho.

A small plane arrived. A man with a Red Cross bag told her she was returning to the United States, as arranged by her mother.

Marita Lorenz married, had another child. After more affairs and more CIA activity, she visited Frank Sturgis in jail. He told her the CIA had killed Camilo Cienfuegos, the man who had saved her life back in Cuba. Based on Sturgis's stories, the *New York Daily* News was preparing a six-part series that would recount the escapades of Marita Lorenz, Superspy. HER CIA ORDERS: KILL FIDEL.

Marita Lorenz, the "curvy, blacked-haired Mata Hari," returned to Cuba one more time in September 1981.

"Welcome back, my little assassin," Castro allegedly said.

She angrily lectured him about the Cuban refugees in Florida, but her animosity couldn't last. They talked about old times, joking about her inability to kill him.

Then Fidel Castro gave her a surprise.

Marita Lorenz was finally introduced to a handsome 22-year-old doctor named Andre, their son.

In 2000 German director Wilfred Huismann made a 92-minute documentary, *Dear Fidel—Marita's Story (Lieber Fidel—Maritas Geschichte),* that recounts this bizarre life story and supports *Der Spiegel*'s observation that "Marita Lorenz claims a respectable share of twentieth-century history for herself."

A CIA HIT (AND MISS) LIST

Using Cuban and American sources, I have compiled a chronological list of 39 other alleged plans and intentions to assassinate Fidel Castro. They don't include unsubstantiated attempts to eliminate Castro when he was a student radical in Havana.

- The first American who hoped to assassinate Fidel Castro was John Maples Spiritto, a CIA official. He stalked Castro in Mexico in 1956 and allegedly confessed to his intentions when he was detained in Cuba in 1962.
- In February 1957, the U.S. ambassador to Cuba, Arthur Gardner, suggested to President Eisenhower that the rebel leader Fidel Castro should be assassinated.
- In 1958, insurrectionist Eutimio Guerra was bribed by Batista's army to kill Castro while he slept in the Sierra Maestra. Guerra chickened out.
- At the behest of organized crime, American Allen Robert Nye landed near Havana in a light plane. He waited with a telescopic rifle in a hotel near the presidential palace, planning to assassinate Castro on February 2, 1959. He was arrested without firing a shot.
- On March 26, 1959, Cuban police uncovered a Castro assassination plan hatched by Batista's information minister, Ernesto de la Fe, and the former head of Batista's death squads, Rolando Masferrer Rojas. Masferrer had fled Cuba by yacht on December 31, 1958. The plan involved another assassination attempt near the presidential palace.

- In a December 11, 1959, memo to Allen Dulles, head of the CIA's Western Hemisphere department, J.C. King proposed the elimination of the Cuban leader who "hypnotically attracts the masses." He later warned that Cuba was not Guatemala and that covert "dirty" tactics were needed to destabilize Castro's regime.

- In February 1960, two Cuban counter-intelligence agents within the U.S. embassy in Havana, Luis Tacornal and José Veiga Peña, learned about plans to kill Castro at the Miramar home of Commander Ramíro Valdés. They received the information from Major Robert Van Horn of the Anti-Communist Workers' Militia and CIA affiliate Lois C. Herber.

- J.C. King recommended on March 9, 1960, that the CIA's task force must "eliminate the leaders with a single blow." The CIA subsequently contrived code names for its assassination targets. As a doctor, Che was known as AMQUACK. Fidel Castro was AMTHUG. In the same month President Eisenhower instructed CIA director Allen Dulles to train Cuban exiles for an invasion of Cuba.

- Roughly between March and September 1960, the CIA experimented with laboratory plans to humiliate or kill Castro. These included thallium powder, to be dusted on his shoes, and lethal cigars. The plan was the powder would make his beard disappear. As well, the CIA considered contaminating the air of the radio station where Castro made his radio speeches with an aerosol spray that would produce results similar to LSD. The CIA experimented with contaminating a box of Castro's favourite brand of cigars with botulinum toxin, poison that would cause death within hours of being ingested. Castro would need to merely place one of these cigars into his mouth to be killed. These cigars were prepared by October 1960 and delivered to an unknown CIA source in February 1961.

- In August 1960 CIA Chief of Operations Richard Bissell requested Colonel Sheffield Edwards, director of the CIA's Office of Security, to find someone to assassinate Castro. Edwards selected former FBI agent Robert Maheu, who had become an aide to Howard Hughes.

- In September 1960, Maheu and Edwards met with underworld figure John Roselli at New York's Plaza Hotel to discuss Castro's assassination. Roselli contacted Chicago crime boss Sam Giancana and the recently deported Havana casino boss Santos Trafficante Jr. of the Florida Mafia. FBI Director J. Edgar Hoover subsequently contacted the CIA's Richard Bissell with a memo (October 18, 1960) to let him know he knew about mobster Sam Giancana's connection to the Castro assassination plot.

- In December 1960 Mafioso John Roselli told the CIA they must devise a plan that would allow a would-be assassin time to escape. Sam Giancana also opposed a gangland slaying with firearms because the killers couldn't escape. In response to Mafia feedback, the CIA's King and Bissell requested the head of their laboratories, Joseph Schreider, to produce poison capsules.

- In January 1961 a young Cuban exile named Félix Rodríguez, among the CIA's Brigade 2506 strike force training in Guatemala, volunteered to assassinate Fidel Castro. He and a companion were flown to Miami where he was given a German-made rifle with a telescopic sight. Rodríguez was then taken to the Cuban coast on three occasions, hoping to shoot Castro in a Havana home, but all attempts failed and the rifle was taken away by the CIA. Félix Rodríguez would eventually oversee the assassination of Che Guevara in Bolivia.

- Soon after John F. Kennedy took office on January 20, 1961, the CIA's Richard Bissell advised National Security Adviser McGeorge Bundy and the CIA's Sidney Gottlieb about plans to assassinate Castro. Bissell and CIA Director Allen Dulles had previously briefed Kennedy about the covert plans to invade Cuba, but not about the assassination plots. Bissell told William Harvey about the need to develop an executive action capability to conduct assassinations. In his notes Harvey quoted Bissell saying to him, "The White House has twice urged me to create such a capability." This executive action capability program was first code-named in CIA files as ZR Rifle in May 1961.

- In February 1961 CIA laboratory chief Joseph Schreider produced little nylon bags with a lethal "synthetic botulism" that dissolved only in cold liquids and left no traces. It also wouldn't take effect on the victim until two or three hours after ingestion. These poisons were given to John Roselli, who then met with Santos Trafficante in Florida. Trafficante contacted Tony Varona, the last president of the Cuban Senate during the administration of President Carlos Prío Socarrás, for help to take the poison to Cuba.

- In the early spring of 1961 Roselli passed the poison pills to Trafficante who had the pills delivered to Juan Orta, a disgruntled Cuban official who no longer received kickbacks from gambling operations. Orta had been chief and director general of the Office of the Prime Minister until January 26, 1961. Orta kept the pills for a few weeks, then returned them. Orta took refuge in the Venezuelan embassy in April. In November he came under the protection of the Mexican embassy when Venezuela broke relations with Cuba. Castro didn't allow Orta to leave Cuba for Mexico City until 1964. He went to Miami in 1965.

- Following Juan Orta's failure, Tony Varona, a.k.a. Dr. Manuel Antonio de Varona y Loredo, met with Trafficante, Roselli, Robert Maheu and Sam Giancana in the Boom-Boom Room of the Fontainbleu in Miami on March 11, 1961. During a televised heavyweight boxing match, Varona accepted their mission to use the poison. Not all participants were fully aware that Varona, as leader of the Democratic Revolutionary Front, was heavily involved in the imminent Bay of Pigs operation. The CIA would pay for Varona's expenses. Unofficially Varona could receive $1 million from the Mafia.

- In March and April 1961, in order to get the poison into Cuba, Varona used a contact of Miami-based Alberto Cruz Caso. The courier was a CIA agent, Alejandro Vergara, subordinated to another CIA agent, Jaime Capdevilla, both of whom were attached to the Spanish embassy. Their plan was to poison Castro at either Havana's Peking Restaurant or else the Havana Libre Hotel, the former Hilton, where Castro sometimes entertained important guests.

- Robert Maheu called John Roselli on April 14, 1961, to report the execution order had been given. But due to the secretive nature required for CIA cover-ups and liaisons, Roselli couldn't locate Varona. Meanwhile, in conjunction with the Bay of Pigs invasion, the Cuban secret service, known as G-2, increased its detention of suspected adversaries. The contact within the Peking Restaurant had subsequently left the country. Castro was far too busy organizing Cuban resistance to the forthcoming invasion to be eating out anyway.

Therefore the contact at Havana Libre received the poison and began to wait for an opportunity to use it.

- As later divulged by CIA operative Humberto Rosales Torres, one of the dates earmarked for assassinations of Fidel Castro and Raúl Castro, as part of the CIA's Operation Patty, was July 26, 1961. The plan included a phoney attack on Guantánamo Naval Base in Cuba that would provide the U.S. with an excuse to send U.S. Marines to Cuba. Operation Patty was foiled when its Cuban leader, Alfredo Izaguirre de la Riva, and his associates were arrested on July 22, 1961.

- In September 1961 Louis Torroella was arrested in Cuba, along with three other men, and charged with planning to assassinate Castro.

- As later divulged by the head of an accounting firm during Batista's regime, Fernando de Royas Penichet, who was recruited by the CIA, October 4, 1961, was one of the scheduled dates to kill Castro, as directed by CIA-sponsored assassins Antonio Veciana Blanch and Bernardo Paradela Ibarreche. Specifically, Antonio Veciana had rented an apartment on the eighth floor at #29 Avenida de las Misiones within 230 feet of the presidential palace's north terrace where Fidel Castro frequently delivered speeches. In preparation for a mass assembly planned to welcome home Cuban president Osvaldo Dorticós from his trip to several socialist countries, Veciana had accumulated a U.S.-made bazooka, hand grenades and machine guns. He and his companions fled to the U.S. the day before, apparently spooked by a conversation with his cousin, a G2 agent. The weapons were discovered and confiscated on October 11.

- In February 1962 the CIA contaminated a box of Castro's favourite cigars with the botulism toxin. The toxin was delivered in pills to Mafioso John Roselli by Colonel Sheffield Edwards. Both schemes went awry.

- In 1962, in conjunction with Operation Mongoose, a propaganda campaign called Operation Botín had packs of chewing gum dropped on the Cuban coastline with pamphlets calling on the Cuban people to assassinate their leaders for a price. The bounty for Fidel Castro was $150,000; for Raúl Castro it was $120,000; and for Che Guevara it was $120,000.

- In January 1963 William Harvey was removed from service in the disbanded Task Force W. In his place, Desmond Fitzgerald was appointed head of the new Special Affairs Service. The SAS devised a more "subtle" plan to assassinate Castro. As an avid scuba diver, Castro would receive scuba equipment infected with the tuberculosis bacillus. This gift would be presented during negotiations for the release of Bay of Pigs prisoners. A suit was prepared with a fungus that would produce a disabling and chronic skin disease, Madura foot, and the breathing apparatus would be contaminated with "tubercle bacilli." This plan was abandoned after it was discovered that the U.S. negotiator for the Bay of Pigs prisoners had already presented Fidel Castro with a diving suit.

- Also in 1963 the CIA considered a scheme to place exploding seashells in two areas where Castro liked to dive. The CIA's Desmond Fitzgerald bought two books on Caribbean molluscs and his plan was seriously considered on several occasions. A midget submarine device would have to be placed within a spectacular "booby-trapped sea shell" that was large enough to catch Castro's eye. An appropriate shell couldn't be found and the operating range of the mini-sub was insufficient.

- In March 1963 Fidel Castro entered the Havana Libre Hotel and asked for a chocolate milk shake. The CIA had delivered poison two years earlier for a barman named Santos de la Caridad. He had been hiding the deadly poison in his dresser at night, removing it carefully in a bag and then placing the capsules inside one of the tubes in the hotel freezer whenever he arrived at work. Castro had visited the Havana Libre Hotel several times, but his visits had never coincided with the barman's shifts. This time the barman nervously began to make the milk shake, preparing the ingredients in the blender, but unusually low refrigeration temperatures that day had caused the capsules to freeze onto the tube and he couldn't remove them. During his efforts to pry them loose, the barman broke the capsules and the poison spilled. Santos de la Caridad brought Fidel Castro his chocolate milk shake as usual. He drank it and went on his way. Santos de la Caridad was arrested the following year along with two other hotel employees. He supposedly confessed and spent several years in jail.

• In October 1963 Special Affairs Service director Desmond Fitzgerald traveled to Paris to confer with Cuban dissident Rolando Cubela Secades, a revolutionary comrade of both Che and Castro. Cubela had been second-in-command of Directionio Revolucionario, a violent anti-Batista group of students who were connected with the assassination of Batista's director of military intelligence in 1956. In 1958 Cubela's DR group was not aligned with Fidel Castro's July 26 Movement. When Che Guevara and Camilo Cienfuegos took over Havana, Cubela and the DR group had been unwilling to cede the presidential palace to Guevara. Cubela's leftists reluctantly handed over the palace to Fidel Castro upon his arrival in Havana. Cubela had become severely dissatisfied with Fidel Castro and was willing to kill him. Fitzgerald subsequently asked CIA laboratories to create a poison pen, the deadly touch of which, on any part of the body, would be so slight as to feel like a mosquito bite.

- Rolando Cubela received the poison pen in a Paris apartment from CIA agent Nestor Sánchez on November 22, 1963. Cubela, a doctor, was not impressed that the CIA had suggested Black Leaf 40 as the poison to be used in the syringe. The telephone rang. The head CIA official in Paris relayed a message to Sánchez that President John Kennedy had just been assassinated in Dallas.

- Cubela returned to Havana with the pen on December 1, 1963. He had been told to wait in Paris after the Kennedy assassination, but he had returned to Cuba via Prague. Cubela had become something of a rogue agent. He demanded a silencer for his Belgian FAL submachine gun in 1964. In December of that year he met the CIA again in Paris, and the two parties understood they were no longer in agreement.

- In December 1964 Cubela met twice in Madrid with Manuel Artime Buesa, a former member of Batista's secret police. E. Howard Hunt had recommended Artime to act as the leader of the Brigade 2506 force that had invaded the Bay of Pigs. Artime agreed to help Cubela obtain an FAL silencer or an equivalent rifle with a silencer. Several months of negotiations and further meetings ensued.

- In February Cubela asked the CIA in Paris for $10,000 to organize an internal coup; the CIA refused and suggested he seek financial help from Artime. Cubela became angry. He was desperately short of funds. The CIA subsequently provided at least three modest payments to Cubela to keep him solvent.

- After more than a year of investigations, Castro stalker Cubela was arrested with his associates in Havana on February 28,

1966. They were planning to shoot Castro with a telescopic rifle. They confessed. The others accused were Ramon Guin Diaz, José Luis Gonzales Gallarreta, Alberto Blanco Romariz and Juan Alsina Navarro. On March 9 Rolando Cubela was sentenced to 25 years.

- On July 18, 1967, Francisco Avila and several other exiles were arrested two days after taking a speedboat to Cuba from Florida, armed with cyanide bullets and high-powered rifles. They were shown on Cuban television in August. Avila was released from prison in 1979 and joined Alpha 66, a terrorist group of anti-Castro exiles based in Florida.

- In November 1971 CIA officials David Phillips and Gerry Hemmings organized an attempt to kill Fidel Castro during his visit with Salvador Allende in Chile. The murder weapon during a press conference in Santiago would be a camera-revolver. The assassination initiative would also encompass Castro's visits to Ecuador and Peru. The operation involved CIA agent Luis Clemente Posada Carriles and Alpha 66 founding member Antonio Veciana, who in July 1973 was arrested on cocaine charges by the U.S. Drug Enforcement Agency. He was sentenced to seven year's imprisonment and served only 17 months.

- Interviewed for Associated Press on May 30, 1975, retired Major General Edward G. Lansdale claimed that President Kennedy had ordered plans to remove Castro, by assassination if necessary, in 1962.

- The CIA planned to kill Castro on his trip to Angola to attend the inauguration ceremonies of the new government on November 11, 1976.

- In July 1981, five Alpha 66 members were captured prior to an assassination attempt on Castro planned for July 26. That same month, Castro charged that the CIA was responsible for an epidemic of dengue fever that killed 81 children. Three years later a dissident named Eduardo Arocena testified that he was a courier for germs brought into Cuba in 1980.

- Cuban counter-revolutionaries planned to assassinate Castro during his visit to Venezuela in 1989.

In 1975 the United States Senate undertook an investigation into American plans for the physical elimination of foreign leaders by the CIA during the 1960s.

This investigation, presided over by Senator Frank Church, was undertaken in the aftermath of the Warren Commission, which had concluded on September 24, 1964, that Lee Harvey Oswald was solely responsible for the assassination of President John F. Kennedy.

The Church report confirmed to the American people that the CIA had three prime assassination targets in the 1960s. These were Patrice Lumumba, the charismatic, leftist leader of the Republic of Congo (murdered by Belgian officials in 1961); Rafael Leonidas Trujillo, an erratic right-wing dictator in the Dominican Republic; and Fidel Castro.

Richard Helms, the CIA director in 1962, testified on June 13, 1975. "I believe it was the policy at the time to get rid of Castro," he said, "and if killing him was one of the things that was to be done in this connection, that was within what was expected."

The Church Committee also confirmed CIA involvement in the assassinations of Mohammed Mossadegh in Iran (1953), Ngo Dinh Diem in South Vietnam (1963) and Chilean General Rene Schneider (1970).

An interim report from the Senate Select Intelligence Committee, November 20, 1975, acknowledged eight CIA plots to kill Castro between 1960 and 1965. As a result President Ford signed an order prohibiting assassinations. Having testified before the Committee about CIA assassination plots, Mafioso John Roselli was later found dead, floating in an oil drum near North Miami Beach.

In 1976 the House of Representatives approved the creation of a House Committee on Assassinations, but not because the American people or American politicians in general had expressed any widespread outrage or dismay at their country's penchant for sponsoring the "physical elimination" of foreign leaders.

The 686-page report of the House Committee on Assassinations was again primarily concerned with the Kennedy assassination. The report timidly suggested that Lee Harvey Oswald had likely not acted alone, and that "evidence does not eliminate the possibility that individual members [of the Mafia] might be involved."

In response to embarrassing, factual columns by U.S. journalist Drew Pearson in early 1967, a confidential CIA Inspector General's Report on plots to assassinate Fidel Castro was compiled in 1967. Declassified in 1994, it frankly documents eight assassination plots and shows how the U.S. government was conspiring with Cuban counter-revolutionaries and the Mafia to "eliminate" Castro. This report confirms that on the same day John F. Kennedy was shot in Dallas, Cuban counter-revolutionary Rolando Cubela was being supplied with a CIA-made, lethal hypodermic pen in Paris to kill Fidel Castro.

There is now corroborative evidence, supplied by Cuba's former head of counter-intelligence, General Fabian Escalante, to support the increasingly widespread contention that individuals who were attempting to orchestrate the murder of Fidel Castro in the 1960s were connected, in varying degrees, to the assassination of John F. Kennedy.

Fidel Castro Family Tree *

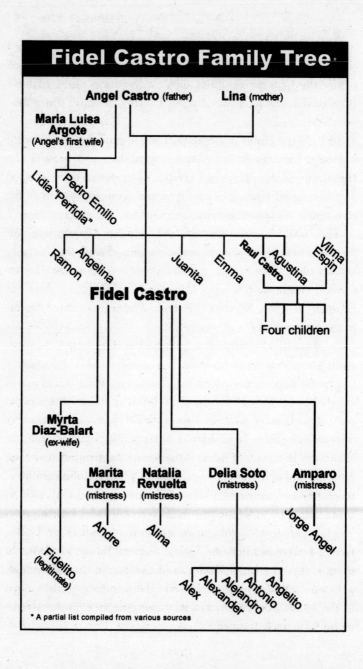

Angel Castro (father)   Lina (mother)

Maria Luisa Argote (Angel's first wife)

Lidia "Perfidia"
Pedro Emilio

Ramon   Angelina   Juanita   Emma   Raul Castro   Agustina   Vilma Espin

Fidel Castro

Four children

Myrta Diaz-Balart (ex-wife)

Marita Lorenz (mistress)   Natalia Revuelta (mistress)   Delia Soto (mistress)   Amparo (mistress)

Andre   Alina   Jorge Angel

Fidelito (legitimate)

Alex   Alexander   Alejandro   Antonio   Angelito

* A partial list compiled from various sources

AUTHOR'S NOTE

I WISH TO EXPRESS MY sincere thanks to all the writers who have gone before me. As a Canadian—and as a Pan-American—I hope *Cuba: A Concise History for Travelers* offers a perspective that is not unduly influenced by either American or Cuban prejudices and ideologies.

There are some excellent guidebooks about Cuba that offer an abundance of advice about eating, sleeping, swimming, music, architecture and money, etc. This book is not a substitute for such practical advice.

Cigars, *mojitos,* beaches, baseball, Hemingway haunts and Tropicana girlie shows are all very well. Enjoy your trip. But be sure to pack 500 years of history with your sunscreen.

That way, you won't get lost.

I started writing this book in 1998 while I was covering Pope John Paul II's historic first Cuban mass in Santa Clara for the *Province* newspaper. When I was stranded for eight hours in a Cuban airport, waiting out a hurricane, I started putting some notes together. Fifty books of research later I hope this primer is both lively and unbiased—the sort of book that might be passed from one visitor to the next.

I've traveled extensively in Cuba, from the off-limits birthplace of El Presidente (where I took the photo of the farmhouse), to the Virgin of Copper church (Cuba's most sacred site), to the seldom-visited landing site for Fidel Castro's ragtag revolutionaries at Playa las Colorados. I've seen compulsory rallies for Elian Gonzalez in Bayamo and visited the Bay of Pigs. I've seen the abandoned Soviet nuclear power plant in Cienfuegos and stood beneath the gigantic Che Guevara memorial in Santa Clara. I've seen the Guantánamo Naval Base and bought trinkets in the postcard-perfect streets of Trinidad. I've gazed at the mists above Pico Turquino and dawdled in the Celia Sánchez museum in Pilón. I saw the Cross of Columbus (allegedly the oldest European relic in the Americas) and explored Cuba's legacy of slavery with a santería *babalawo* (medium) in El Cobre (site of the oldest, continually operational open-pit mine in the Americas).

All of which is left out of this book.

The best discoveries are those you will make for yourself. I hope this book succeeds in helping you discover your own version of Cuba.

Havana street scene, 2000

BIBLIOGRAPHY

The quotations used in this book come from some of the following sources:

Anderson, Jon Lee. *Che Guevara: A Revolutionary Life.* New York: Grove Press, 1997.

Arenas, Reinaldo. *Before Night Falls, A Memoir.* New York: Viking Penguin, 1993.

Baker, Christopher P. *Cuba Passport.* Emeryville: Moon Publications, 1997.

Barclay, Juliet. *Havana: Portrait of a City.* London: Cassell, 1993.

Benítez-Rojo, Antonio. *The Repeating Island.* Durham: Duke University Press, 1992.

Betto, Frei. *Fidel & Religion.* Melbourne: Ocean Press, 1990.

Bourne, Peter. *A Biography of Fidel Castro.* New York: Dodd, Mead, 1986.

Cabrera Infante, Guillermo. *Mea Cuba.* London: Farrar, Straus & Giroux, 1994.

Castro, Fidel. *History Will Absolve Me.* Ediciones Politicas, Editorial de Ciencias Sociales. Havana: Cuban Book Institute, 1975.

CIA Targets Fidel: Secret 1967 CIA Inspector General's Report on Plots to Assassinate Fidel Castro. Melbourne: Ocean Press, 1996.

Coe, Andrew. *Cuba.* Chicago: Passport Books, 1997.

Collier, Peter, and David Horowitz. *The Kennedys: An American Drama.* New York: Summit Books, 1984.

Crankshaw, Edward. *Khrushchev: A Career.* New York: Viking, 1966.

Debray, Régis. *Prison Writings.* Markham, ON: Penguin Books, 1975.

Face to Face with Fidel Castro: A Conversation with Tomás Borge. Melbourne: Ocean Press, 1993.

Fernández, Alina. *Castro's Daughter: An Exile's Memoir of Cuba.* New York: St. Martin's Press, 1998.

Franklin, Jane. *Cuba and the United States: A Chronological History.* Melbourne: Ocean Press, 1997.

Furiati, Claudia. *ZR Rifle: The Plot to Kill Kennedy and Castro.* Melbourne: Ocean Press, 1994.

Geyer, Georgie Anne. *Guerrilla Prince: The Untold Story of Fidel Castro.* Kansas City: Little, Brown, 1991.

Gimbel, Wendy. *Havana Dreams: A Story of Cuba.* New York: Vintage Random House, 1998.

Guevara, Che. *Che Guevara Speaks: Selected Speeches and Writings.* Ed. G. Lavan. Nigeria and Havana: Zim Pan African Publishers and José Martí Publishing House, 1988.

Halperin, Maurice. *The Taming of Fidel Castro.* Berkeley: University of California Press, 1979.

Hartmann Matos, Alejandro. *Les Francais a Baracoa.* Valencia: 1999.

———. *Los Días de Colón en Baracoa.* Valencia: 1995.

Holt-Seeland, Inger. *Women of Cuba.* Westport: Lawrence Hill & Co. Inc., 1982.

Hungry Wolf, Adolf. *Letters from Cuba.* Skookumchuck: Canadian Caboose Press, 1996.

———. *Trains of Cuba,* Skookumchuck: Canadian Caboose Press, 1996.

Iyer, Pico. *Cuba and the Night.* New York: Knopf, 1995.

Lewis, Oscar, Ruth M. Lewis and Susan Rigdon. *Four Men: Living the Revolution, An Oral History of Contemporary Cuba.* Chicago: University of Illinois Press, 1977.

Lorenz, Marita, and Ted Schwarz. *Marta: One Woman's Extraordinary Tale of Love and Espionage from Castro to Kennedy.* Berkeley: Thunder's Mouth Press, 1993.

Moore, Marjorie, and Adrienne Hunter. *Seven Women and the Cuban Revolution.* Havana: Lugus Publications, 1997.

Pendle, George. *A History of Latin America.* Baltimore: Penguin, 1963.

Pérez, Louis A., Jr. *The War of 1898: The United States and Cuba in History and Historiography.* Chapel Hill: University of North Carolina Press, 1999.

Perrottet, Tony, and Joann Biondi, eds. *Cuba.* Concord: APA Publications, Houghton Mifflin, 1996.

Ponce de León, Juana, and Esteban Ríos Rivera, eds. *Dream with No Name: Contemporary Fiction from Cuba.* New York: Seven Stories Press, 1999.

Reporting on Cuba. Havana: Ensayo Book Institute Havana, 1967.

Ripley, C. Peter. *Conversations with Cuba.* Athens, GA: University of Georgia Press, 1999.

Ryan, Alan, ed. *The Reader's Companion to Cuba.* New York: Harcourt Brace & Company, 1997.

Simons, Geoff. *Cuba: From Conquistador to Castro.* New York: St. Martin's Press, 1996.

Soldevila, Carlos. *Cuba.* Montreal: Ulysseys Travel Publications, 1997.

Stanley, David. *Cuba.* Hawthorn, Australia: Lonely Planet, 1997.

Szulc, Tad. *Fidel: A Critical Portrait.* New York: William Morrow, 1986.

Tagliattini, Maurizio. "The Discovery of North America." 1998.

Thomas, Hugh. *Cuba: The Pursuit of Freedom.* San Francisco: Harper & Row, 1971.

Ward, Fred. *Inside Cuba Today.* New York: Crown Publishers, 1978.

Williams, Diana. *Diving and Snorkeling Guide to Cuba.* Houston: Pisces Books, 1996.

Willinsky, John. *Learning to Divide the World: Education at Empire's End.* Minneapolis: University of Minnesota Press, 1998.

Yebra Garcia, Rita María. *All Havana.* Havana: Com-Relieve, S.A. y Editorial Escudo de Oro, S.A., fourth edition, undated.

In addition, the author has consulted many periodicals, chiefly the *Guardian Weekly, New Yorker, Granma* (English editions) and Amnesty International reports.

INDEX

TRAVELER'S NOTES AND ADDRESSES